BEHIND THE SCHOOLHOUSE DOORS

AN OBSESSION WITH A YOUNG STUDENT

BERNARD H. COHEN

ISBN: 1482048310
ISBN-13: 9781482048315
Library of Congress Control Number: 2013901418
CreateSpace Independent Publishing Platform
North Charleston, South Carolina

For abused children; may they recover and shine.

PREFACE

Before the Penn State sex abuse scandal tore at the fiber of that university and the entire sports world, Bob Parkman shocked the city of Clearwater, New York, and America's entire education community with the first-ever sexual molestation of a student by an American School Superintendent.

In this bizarre but true story, a successful education leader and family man with five children becomes obsessed with a 12-year-old boy. This impacted the lives of many children, their teachers, parents and school administrators in the Hudson Valley city of Clearwater, New York.

I was Principal of Clearwater High School, when my boss, School Superintendent Robert Parkman, became obsessed with a boy named Seth, and was eventually jailed for child sex abuse. Vulnerable in many ways due to economic, academic and personal challenges, Seth was a defenseless target for a man who won the trust of a city and designed his life to appear ordinary and conventional, the classic Jekyll-Hyde.

I came to Clearwater from New York City where I was a long-time Harlem and South Bronx administrator specializing in turning around failing schools. Clearwater High School needed a leader who could swim in the deep water with the under-achieving urban kids and keep both hands on the wheel when the road was rocky. I was that guy. It was a dream job for a principal entering the autumn of an already exciting career. My challenge was to renew the High School to its former glory and to lead a talented teaching team, most of whom were on staff when I arrived.

Superintendent Parkman came to Clearwater from West Virginia via western New York. He professed to be a man of faith and he decorated his home with crucifixes. His favorite Superintendent activity was reading to young kids on National Reading Day. Parkman dressed and acted in most ways you'd expect from a School Superintendent. An upstanding citizen, he paid his taxes on time and enjoyed visiting the nearby West Point Cadets.

Parkman's obsessive behaviors, the sexual acts, the unusual confrontations and all that happens in Behind The Schoolhouse Doors are based on my direct observation or the sworn testimony of others. All verbal quotes are accurate and the newspaper articles are authentic, although redacted and shortened. Any personal thoughts attributed to characters in this story, unless taken from testimony or other record, are my own interpretations and are clearly distinct from testimony and observations throughout the book.

It is important to share the events comprising this and other stories such as the Penn State fiasco, to recount how pedophiles often establish themselves within a protective framework that includes a legitimate source of prey. Parents and teachers need to address school district governance procedures and, for that matter, the governance procedures of most public agencies which inadvertently provide access and protection to potential child abusers.

The names of people in this book have been changed, with the exception of my attorney's name and my own, due to an agreement I made with the School District. The agreement was aimed at protecting the District from further harm beyond what this Superintendent and the incident have already caused. The School District name has also been changed because the lessons learned from this episode matter more than the location.

Bernard H. Cohen

Acknowledgements

I dedicate this book to all the victims of child-molesters; to the sexually-violated child in this horrendous story and to the many children targeted by perverted Jekyll-Hydes working and preying in education where child-contact is a normal part of the work and wholesome virtues easily mask deviance.

I dedicate this truth to my parents who gave me the values upon which my decisions herein were made, and particularly my father who, without knowing, molded me to meet and overwhelm the challenges of this case. He initiated, followed by me after his death, the first asbestos lawsuit against 13 manufacturers. We combined to fight in a court battle for 18 years, a case which has since become a class action that has benefited over a 100,000 Navy Yard asbestos victims.

"The Truth Shall Make Us Free" was pasted all over Adelphi University as its motto. That was important to me after winning a full scholarship to a new life; interacting with professors who motivated me to triple major in education, theatre and biology. I am still motivated by them to think inter-disciplinarily.

I dedicate this book to Chris Watkins, my attorney, who devotes his professional life to fighting for those wrongly terminated or otherwise abused by their employers. I shouldn't tell you this, but he has a big red cape under his lawyer clothes and a big red "S" on his undershirt.

I also thank my family and personal friends for enduring the stress of this prolonged effort, especially my daughter who is now a teacher and school administrator, but was taking graduate courses nearby during very public aspects of this case, and had to handle professor and student curiosities on a regular basis.

Finally, I thank, Wendy Wetstein Czerwinski, my assistant. She pushed, prodded and continuously held up a standard for the book that would not let us compromise the story or the quality of our presentation.

PART I

CHAPTER 1

Seth's hands trembled. His entire body shivered with fear as he called Bob's cell phone. He knew their age difference was extreme, but Bob's lavish gifts and attention were more than he could ignore. Anyway, tonight, he wasn't calling to say "thanks."

Seth's new friend, Robinson, saw him shudder as the call went through, and put a reassuring hand on his shoulder. Although Seth had called Bob hundreds of times, tonight would be different. Now 14 years old and in high school, Seth finally gave in to the incessant prodding of Robinson and others, and was ready to end his relationship with Bob.

Seventh and eighth grade classmates had teased Seth about Bob. Seth's family and teachers had chastised him for being best friends with Bob, a middle-aged man. Even Seth's normally-docile father finally questioned and forbade the two-year relationship, but Bob ignored him by delivering a Christmas basket of expensive gift certificates.

That act of defiance, when all had agreed to a separation, convinced Seth that Bob was a seductive manipulator. Bob's gift basket, ignoring Seth's father, catalyzed the young boy to unleash himself from the older man's grip.

Seth's name appeared on Bob's caller ID. Although it was a cold January night, Bob rushed outside to the patio for privacy. Before Bob could even answer, Seth was speaking at his usual rapid pace.

"Hey, Bob, it's Seth. What's going on? You haven't called me in weeks. Mrs. Lewis brought me a note from you that said we are in a trial separation and she said that you miss me. I understand the separation but I'd really like to get together tonight. I think we have something great to celebrate and I really appreciate the Christmas gifts."

"What are we celebrating," Bob asked, huddled against the cold Hudson Valley wind, ready to end the imposed separation.

Seth refused to answer about the celebration. Instead, he teased.

"I'll share that information when we're together."

Seth had been nervous about calling, but the sound of Bob's voice temporarily re-assured him. But, again Seth's body trembled. He abruptly ended the call, promising to call back in ten minutes.

Bob was curious about the unexpected celebration and excited about the renewed relationship. After ten minutes, Seth called.

"The reason for celebrating is so important," Seth teased, "that only sex should end this wonderful day. My father will be staying overnight at Grandma's because she's sick."

Bob pushed him. "If we're going to have sex, you've got to tell me what we're celebrating," He followed with his usual counsel.

"You know, Seth, I always leave the sex stuff up to you."

Seth wanted no misunderstanding.

"Bob, I mean *real sex* tonight."

"Like I said, Seth, I always leave that up to you; real sex or not, whatever."

Again, Seth got nervous.

"All the lights will be out in my house. If any lights are on, don't stop to pick me up. That means my father came home." Bob responded with a promise of real sex "like before."

Seth closed the phone. No longer nervous, the high school sophomore now felt sick, thinking of all the sex he had with a 54-year-old man.

On the other end, Bob made excuses to his family for his unexpected evening departure. His household only included 17-year-old daughter, Lynn, and his wife, Linda. Bob's other children were adults, living out-of-town or away at college.

Bob wasn't thinking about his family. He'd been pining for Seth during a separation that was imposed by the boy's father after the police and I convinced him to be more concerned about his son's relationship with Bob.

Bob's family, also concerned, had long-pressured him about Seth. Bob ignored them and described his inter-generational relationship as mentoring.

"If Seth could realize that I was like him at his age and that I grew up to be successful, I could be a role model for him."

CHAPTER 2

I was Seth's high school principal, responsible for educating and protecting 2,000 students and for supervising 250 staff. Unfortunately, I slowly became the narrator of an emerging scandalous child abuse case. Seth joined us as a high school freshman after a year that had already been momentous. In my third year as Principal, Clearwater High School withstood the World Trade Center tragedy, anthrax scares and a TB-find that required weeks of student and staff screening by the Health Department. That same school year, we also experienced two student deaths and the murder of a beloved guidance counselor. We handled all those socio-emotional challenges but could not protect one boy, Seth, from his middle-aged boyfriend because Bob was our School District Superintendent, our boss.

Seth's phone call that night, after weeks of forced separation, caught Bob off-guard.

"I'll do anything for you tonight. I want to help you celebrate whatever it is you're so up about. My Snake wants you but first we'll make sure Banana feels good," Bob told him, using code words he'd made up for their penises.

Seth had him hooked. Now, to reel him in.

"You can pick me up but only if you promise we're gonna have sex tonight like last month."

"Yes, yes, yes," Bob responded, "we'll have sex like before, good sex."

Bob grabbed his coat while shouting "goodbye" to his family, giving them a list of errands he needed to complete. How could his family complain about errands?

"I'm going to the bank, getting gas in the car, mailing bills and picking up some things for my office at the supermarket."

There were no questions.

Bob sorely missed Seth. Several days earlier, after only ten days of the imposed separation, he came to my office and locked the door behind him. The Superintendent was always chubby and wore suits that were either too tight or too large. This day, he wore a light gray plaid suit left-over from his days in West Virginia. It had a rural quality and looked silly in Clearwater.

"I've given that boy more in two years than his family gave him during the previous 12 years, but people around here cannot accept that my mentoring has turned into an inter-generational friendship. They are forcing us not to see each other." This was several days before Seth's alluring phone call. Tears rolled from Bob's eyes as he snapped a tissue from the box on my conference table. They were not crocodile tears. He sobbed. His chubby face turned pink. His eyes reddened.

"Without me to protect this special child from insensitive teachers and his n'er do well father, he will not survive," he added, through a steady stream of tears. Bob had become vulnerable in his loneliness for Seth. The late-night phone call caught him very needy.

As he drove the few minutes from his high-end neighborhood to Seth's house, Bob must have congratulated himself for buying Seth a cell phone. Their private conversations could avoid eavesdroppers at both ends.

Seth watched for Bob's car on the dark street and met him at the curb.

"Wait in the car. I'll be right back," he said.

Bob watched Seth jump the steps to the small house that was in great disrepair. He often told me how disgusted he was by Seth's father's inability to improve their financial circumstances. The rented house was a small two-story colonial with white paint peeling and an overgrown lawn. It was only steps from large commercial and manufacturing buildings on a main street. It was the kind of house usually rented cheaply until further development made it profitable to demolish.

When Seth re-entered the darkened house, he was greeted in whispers by his new friend, Detective Robinson of the Clearwater Police.

"Does he suspect anything?"

"He's been only thinking of sex since the first phone call you taped tonight," Seth answered.

Judge Harold Fredericks had approved a wiretap on Seth's cell phone after the 14-year old finally, after two years of our hounding, revealed that he had sexual activities with our School Superintendent.

Robinson whispered to Seth, "You did the right thing in coming to us. Now let us take over." Robinson had his badge hanging from the outside pocket of his dark suit. In his locally-known, crisp "Bogie" manner, Robinson radioed Lieutenant Foster and Lieutenant Somerset.

"The eagle is alone in the front. The egg is back in the nest with me. Pick him up."

After hearing "roger" from Foster and Somerset, Detective Robinson left the house and hopped down the front steps. Foster's unmarked car sped around the corner to form a roadblock ten feet in front of the car driven by School Superintendent Robert Parkman, whose life as he knew it was ending.

Parkman quickly recognized Detective Robinson running toward him from the house, even in darkness. A veteran in Clearwater's Youth Crime Division, Robinson was that year's "Detective of the Year" for the eight-county Hudson Valley region, prior to this shocking arrest.

Just as Parkman recognized Robinson, he also saw the speeding car bursting around the corner of his periphery to block his forward progress. He threw his car into reverse to make a panicky escape around Foster's car but Lieutenant Somerset had simultaneously parked behind him, allowing an arrest that would throw an entire city into shock and turmoil for years.

The $150,000 a year School Superintendent did not resist when Foster directed, "get out of your car, sir, and keep your hands in full view." These cops' own children were under Parkman's daily responsibility. They controlled themselves.

Dressed now in jeans, a sweater and a short winter jacket, the Superintendent gave them a pathetic feigned puzzled look, informing them, "I am Bob Parkman, School Superintendent, and I'm . . ."

"Please step around behind your car, so we can tell you why you're under arrest," Robinson sternly interrupted.

Somerset, who had considered Parkman a church friend, was more polite, "I'm sorry to do this to you, sir, but you must put your hands behind you so I can put the handcuffs on." Parkman complied and became the first sitting American School Superintendent arrested for sexually molesting one of his students.

With his pink, fleshy face held down firmly on the trunk of his school district car, and his ample stomach pressed into the car's rear end, the handcuff pain was the least of the Superintendent's problems and went unnoticed by him except for the initial pinch.

CHAPTER 3

Parkman had repeatedly told me how his children and wife begged him to get Seth out of his life. His family loved him and accepted his many idiosyncrasies, but having an adolescent for a close friend stretched their tolerance. Although Bob thought about his family when the police surrounded him, those thoughts faded from this new reality when the handcuffs snapped shut.

Parkman had already lost his father, a former Air Force pilot who died several years earlier.

"My father wanted a macho-man for a son and was disappointed when I became a teacher, a woman's profession, in his opinion," Parkman told me after his father's funeral.

As Parkman lay handcuffed on the trunk of his car, he had to be relieved that his father would miss this spectacle. The humiliation his father would have borne from the sodomy and other charges recited by Robinson on that cold January street, would have been grounds for paternal disownment, especially with the victim being a boy.

When the handcuffs snapped closed, Bob must have thought about Seth and wondered how much pressure it took to make him disclose their sexual relationship. Where had he gone so wrong that Seth should betray him?

After a quick police search of his vehicle which he always proudly proclaimed "crispy clean," Bob responded:

"There's nothing in my car that allows you to arrest me . . . I am the School Superintendent. You must release me immediately . . . You are confusing me with someone else."

What else *could* he say! Robinson and Somerset had the last word.

"You are under arrest for sexual abuse of a minor, sodomizing a minor and other charges based on judge-authorized phone tapes earlier this evening. In those calls you were overheard discussing your sexual relationship with Seth."

Detective Robinson informed the Superintendent of his rights and told him they would immediately go to the Parkman home where a judge-approved search for evidence was already underway in front of his wife and daughter.

Hours earlier, when the judge granted permission to tape phone conversations, I received separate confidential calls from three Clearwater cops with whom I'd worked on this case. Each told me he was on the way to bust Parkman. I was involved with them, investigating the man-boy relationship, for 18 months until today, when Seth's disclosure resulted in an arrest within hours.

Parkman's family fit comfortably into their upwardly mobile neighborhood along with the doctors, lawyers, and other high-income professionals. His yard backed onto a large wooded park which he often described as his secret forest hideaway. He enjoyed watching for unusual birds and using the park as a full-scale nature classroom for his walks with Seth.

To most observers, Parkman seemed socially awkward but he was totally at ease with nature, especially bird-watching. He was proud of owning several animal drawings by one of the country's foremost wildlife artists who happened to live in Pottstown, New York where Parkman was a district administrator prior to his Clearwater Superintendency. He had moved to Pottstown after being a middle school principal in West Virginia.

When I joined the Clearwater School District, Parkman gave me a personal tour of his now-invaded house. He emphasized the natural surroundings of the adjacent park, but he was also thrilled about his designer bathroom which included totally mirrored walls and ceilings. The outwardly proper School Superintendent indulged himself during that house tour with a few mirror-fantasy jokes that were totally out-of-sync with local perception of his staid personality. Knowing him less than a month, the jokes were off-putting.

After showing off the mirrored bathroom, Parkman proudly opened his walk-in closet which was more like a dressing room than a closet. It included a full dresser, mirror, and window facing the front lawn. During the closet tour, he explained how neighborhood boys watched through the window as he dressed each morning. Even before meeting Seth, he thought the local boys wanted to emulate him because he was their Superintendent.

"They really care about my personal habits and attire," he told me. "The boys wait across the street for the school bus and watch me dress when it's dark outside and the closet lights are on, but I don't care."

When I jokingly teased him about the value of boys seeing him select his shirts and ties, he got defensive. He didn't like the joking.

"I'm not going to change my habits because they're watching. I don't like to close the blinds," he said, foreshadowing events I could not then imagine.

Other than those few odd comments, Parkman seemed to be living in a well-designed, 1950's, Ozzie and Harriet-styled setting.

Early in my tenure in Clearwater, I could see that Parkman had the knowledge but had neither the savoir-faire nor the confidence of a School Superintendent. On the contrary, he was more like an adult nerd, a grown-up child. His awkwardness was especially noticeable in social settings, particularly in the presence of other Superintendents. He despised the monthly Superintendents' meetings he was forced to attend with 16 other Hudson Valley Superintendants. After we became friends, he'd ask me to call him during those meetings so he could leave for a supposed "Clearwater crisis." This puzzled me. I respected his anti-establishment sentiments but I also knew those meetings were important.

At regional events with other Superintendents, such as the annual dinner honoring area high school valedictorians, he'd insist I sit with him so he'd not have to be sociable with board members or parents of the honored students. He'd always make sure our table was the first to leave.

Parkman was a gadget-geek, as well as a social nerd, always looking for the latest in electronics which might allow him to be "The Superintendent of Oz," running the school district from behind an electronic curtain, avoiding personal contact with teachers and parents. He was more comfortable using electronic communications than summoning up phony charisma or rhetoric, neither of which fit well. His lifeless, annual welcome-speeches to staff were always the butt of jokes behind his back. His graduation speeches were inane, often comprised of little more than internet lists, such as "Things People Born in 1985 Never Did." Public speaking was an emotional challenge for him. He understood shy people and empathized with them. You wondered how he became a Superintendent with the leadership style of TV's Mr. Rogers.

The real leadership personality in Clearwater's administration was Donald Ross, one of Parkman's Assistant Superintendents. His office was ten feet from Parkman's and he was the educational brains of the School District. In fact, his long-range plan was the main reason I left the excitement of New York City.

Ross had the high energy Parkman lacked, and he lured me to the District with his desire to cure the District's failing schools with creative initiatives. Prior to joining Clearwater as their high school principal, my success in turning-around failing schools had been widely publicized. After Ross visited my school in the Bronx, he asked me to lead Clearwater High School which had experienced a two-decade slide.

Ross met with Parkman upon returning from my school, emphasizing my leadership skills and the manner in which I'd engendered support from a diverse population, including the teachers' union, no small feat for an administrator. Parkman wanted to meet me but was concerned I'd be "too independent to supervise."

Ross advised me before my meeting with Parkman: "Don't be too strong a personality or too independent or too smart because you'll frighten him." Even though I was forewarned, Parkman's opinion of me was negative.

"Difficult to supervise, too independent to follow guidelines, and too outspoken for Clearwater." He was right about all these things.

Ross persuaded Parkman to hire me.

"You need a veteran to lead that high school because it is out-of-control. You need somebody who will go into that school, kick butt and take names; somebody who's not afraid of the bad boys or the bad teachers." He was convinced and I was hired.

CHAPTER 4

While Detective Robinson and his partners arrested Parkman, eight police cars and vans descended on the Parkman family at their home. They were advised of his arrest and shown a search warrant. The yard took on the appearance of a movie set with floodlights shining through the darkness on every corner of the house.

How did it get to this point, Parkman's wife thought, as she watched police remove his computer and cartons of potentially damaging evidence, including bed linens and sofa cushions for DNA examination. His family did not visit Parkman in jail that night. Instead, they left town to stay with relatives. He had ignored their pleas. They now ignored him.

Stories quickly surfaced regarding Parkman and Seth's first meeting. Descriptions of that first encounter were often designed to protect whoever was telling the story. Nobody wanted to be linked to their first meeting.

Seth's pre-trial deposition addressed the initial meeting and was not kind to the Middle School. Seth testified:

"I told some people at my school that I was being harassed by a school staff member. After my complaint was ignored, I requested a meeting with the Superintendent."

"Go ahead if that's what you want," the 12-year old was told, according to his testimony.

Nobody thought the boy would follow-through; however, Seth telephoned the Superintendent's secretary and arranged to present his complaint to Parkman.

The seventh grader arrived at Parkman's office wearing a dark blue suit, white shirt and tie. He had combed his hair in a mature style and immediately impressed the Superintendent with his showcase manners, his unusual etiquette, and his kowtowing respect for authority. Parkman also liked Seth's very mature vocabulary and his keen interest in the technology which filled the room.

Parkman immediately appreciated aspects of Seth that others derided; good manners and respect for authority. These were soothing balms to Parkman in an otherwise often-contentious job. The children Parkman usually met were among the more difficult to manage. Seth appeared more Ghandi-like to Parkman than the children he usually met.

Seth told Parkman about the complaints he had made to his school. Parkman listened intently.

"I have now told my school three times that I was sexually harassed by a staff member and the last time it was because he called me a "faggot.'"

Seth was also ingratiating.

"I know how busy you must be, so I understand if this is something you want to turn over to somebody else. I apologize for using your time on something as insignificant as this." Parkman was impressed by the 12-year old and told him so.

Seth spoke with a grammar beyond his age, making Parkman think Seth was the middle school class president or other outstanding achiever.

Upon hearing Seth's complaint, Parkman telephoned the Middle School. Smitten by Seth's demeanor, the Superintendent impressed the boy by using the speakerphone.

When the Middle School folks heard Seth had gone to the Superintendent, they laughed derisively, according to Seth's testimony. Parkman did not tell the Middle School they were on speakerphone.

"We can't believe that nut actually showed up. We're sorry, Bob. We did not think he would actually show up at your office to bother you. Is his crazy father with him? We're really sorry, Bob. We never thought - "

"Enough!" Parkman yelled, knowing Seth could hear what they said, "I'll discuss this with you later."

The speakerphone incident quickly brought Seth and Parkman into a confidential relationship. When the call ended, Parkman apologized to Seth, who was thrilled to have the Superintendent of Schools hear how disrespectfully he had been treated. Parkman then complimented Seth's vocabulary and etiquette, both of which had been objects of bullying at school.

"Here's my card. You may call me direct if you need me or if you just want to talk." The pains of his own childhood gave 54-year-old Parkman a reason to quickly identity with Seth. Parkman had told me that any child's social awkwardness struck a familiar chord with him; "I see myself in them at that age."

Before their first meeting ended, they played with the Superintendent's computer for an hour until Parkman's secretary reminded him of an appointment.

"Let's go. I'll drive you back to school now."

During the few blocks to the Middle School, Seth had a non-stop stream of consciousness about his new friendship. He later told NBC, "I suddenly felt I have a powerful friend, I have a friend who has access. My new friend has everything I could possibly want." He told Kendra Farr, the reporter, "the School Superintendent reacted to me differently than any other adult. Here was the Superintendent of Schools, the most powerful person in my experience, taking an interest in me. I was so impressed."

CHAPTER 5

The Police Department answering machine informed callers: "You have reached the Juvenile Division and Crime Prevention Unit of the Clearwater Police Department. If you would like to leave a message for Lieutenant Somerset or Detective Robinson, please do that at the sound of the beep."

Before Seth completed middle school, several teachers and local restaurateurs left anonymous messages on this answering machine, messages about Parkman doting unprofessionally on the boy. Clearwater residents were hyper-sensitive about educators fraternizing with students. Police records show four Clearwater staff had been arrested for child molestation in the five years prior to Parkman's arrival.

A full-time school district doctor was arrested after he sexually molested more than a dozen elementary school boys in his school office. He served time in an upstate New York prison. After his release, he was later jailed for leaving the country for the purpose of having sex with minors.

About the same time, a Clearwater High School special education teacher was arrested after she engaged in sexual intercourse with several teenagers at her Clearwater home. She also served jail time and subsequently snuck into a school district job in upstate New York until she was reported by Clearwater teachers who met her at an education conference.

A Clearwater High School science teacher was also jailed after having sex with several local students. After serving jail time, he relocated to Florida, was hired as a science teacher and again jailed after having sex with underage Florida students. These and other sexual violations by Clearwater faculty, sensitized locals to a heightened degree.

"Lieutenant Somerset, I own a local restaurant that shall be nameless at this time because I want to report that our School Superintendent brought a young boy to breakfast on several recent Sundays and it just didn't look right . . ."

"Lieutenant Somerset, I am a teacher at the Middle School and I'm not happy to report that our School Superintendent is removing one of our male students from the building on a fairly regular basis, at least three or four times per month and, in addition, the boy visits the Superintendent in his office."

The Superintendent had quickly become obsessed with his new middle school friend. He visited Seth's school to speak with his teachers whenever Seth complained about any of them. Parkman also transferred the individual who taunted Seth.

The Superintendent immersed himself in Seth's academic history, learning that Seth was an under-achieving student in comparison to his high intelligence. Parkman told me he wanted to improve Seth's reading and help him face challenges better. Because Parkman's experience as a teacher had been limited to higher-level students learning foreign languages, and his own high-achieving children, he had no understanding of any child's academic or emotional challenges.

At first, Parkman's involvement seemed like legitimate mentoring to the Middle School teachers. His counsel always focused on academic progress and Seth's personal management. However, the tone of their discussions soon convinced teachers that Parkman was too emotionally involved with Seth and they were concerned when Parkman began removing Seth from school.

A Middle School teacher and a counselor later testified they telephoned anonymous reports to Somerset's answering machine. One staff member testified that he was warned to, "Keep your mouth shut about Parkman or he'll transfer you."

Seth completed seventh grade with Parkman's constant academic help and emotional support. Parkman became so emotionally involved with Seth's academic life that he suffered his own personal angst with each of Seth's tests or homework assignments. The Superintendent started calling me to complain about the "huge amount of homework teachers were assigning." I thought he was complaining about his daughter's teachers at my school. I even stopped her "randomly" in the corridor to ask her and several of her friends about the hours they were devoting to nightly assignments. But, Parkman was only concerned about Seth's assignments. I had not yet learned about him and Seth.

After seventh grade ended, it was no longer "Mr. Parkman," but "Bob." Seth accompanied Bob during weekend errands and called Bob to "rescue" him from his problematic household. About that time, Seth's mother left home to live with a man she met on the internet, leaving three children and a husband.

Seth's Dad was employed on a part-time basis at a local Kwik-Stop deli/gas station. With Mom's income now gone, the family subsisted at a poverty level. Having three children who needed extra care and personal attention, prevented Dad from working even part-time.

Seth's wheelchair-bound older sister had cerebral palsy and his younger sister also had health issues. They wore clothes from a thrift shop and ate meals at a barely nutritional level. Dad rallied the family every evening by focusing on a televised science fiction series, "River of Fire." This gave them a nightly bonding experience and an unusual vocabulary.

Seth made many of the household decisions that summer. Dad was busy caring for his ailing mother in a nearby town, leaving Seth as family caretaker.

These circumstances made Bob's home and his attention very attractive. When Dad was home, Seth would leave for Parkman's home. He spent many hours at the Parkman's during the summer prior to eighth grade.

Teachers, restaurant owners and other locals continued to leave concerned messages on the police voicemail. None reported anything sexual or illegal. No public display of affection was ever described. People only spoke of sensing an unusual closeness, a giddiness or strange friendship, an inappropriate casualness for two unrelated males 40 years apart in age.

Clearwater police conducted interviews with several teachers and a school security guard, but never filed reports about these early calls and interviews because the "small town" aspects of Clearwater would mitigate against secrecy. Police later testified about managing the entire case without filing any reports due to their fear of leaks.

Police even directed me to file no official school or police reports when I became involved. They strongly believed such reports would have prevented them from catching Parkman, were he guilty. In testimony, Somerset pointed out that Parkman's secretaries had close relatives in the Police Department and he worried about leaks that could have reached Parkman.

CHAPTER 6

Bob and Seth's playful summer did not do much to ease Seth's annual bout of August stress when school-opening loomed. He was facing another year of academic struggle and social pain. In second grade he was scheduled to be evaluated to determine if he needed academic support. His mother refused the testing and provided her own academic support for Seth. But, six years later, eighth grade loomed large and mom was no longer there to help Seth begin the year.

Increasing financial and homemaking demands kept Dad in a near frenzy while Seth and Bob grew closer. The Superintendent counseled his young friend into eighth grade, filling-in for Mom.

To avoid athletic humiliation, Seth leaned toward intellectual recreation, but his reading skills did not keep pace with his intellectual development. Testing, re-testing and constant evaluation became part of Seth's life because of the discrepancy between his high intelligence and his achievement.

Dad realized that Seth had excellent spoken-language skills and a high-level vocabulary. He explained that Seth could hear a spoken word in context and correctly use it in later conversation.

As a result, television films became Seth's language-learning tool, giving him the sophisticated vocabulary which Parkman mistook for maturity. Seth heard sophisticated words in a film and could use them appropriately. Adults were impressed, but his peers were turned-off.

Parkman told me, "My own kids didn't have problems so I've been oblivious to this kind of testing and labeling. The American education system has failed Seth so I will teach him." Although Parkman sounded sincere at the time, I now know he was setting a trap for an innocent boy already facing serious issues.

Seth's interest in Bob's computer was matched by Bob's interest in solving Seth's problems. There was a mutual eagerness. Their meetings started with tech-talk but would always include discussions about Seth's personal life. Parkman thrived on solving Seth's academic and personal problems. Their needs were perfect for each other, except that Seth was 12 years old and Parkman was 54 with a wife and children.

The Superintendent's family was the all-American success story. Parkman was School Superintendent of Clearwater after being an administrator in Pottstown, New York. Before that, he was a middle school principal in West Virginia after years as a Spanish teacher. His children were successful and problem-free. His wife was involved in community activities and shared Bob's strong faith and close family ties. But, she worried about her husband's obsession with Seth from the start.

After his arrest, Clearwater newspaper reporters explored Parkman's past and visited his former school districts to find reasons for his departure from earlier jobs. In West Virginia, they uncovered concerns about Parkman kissing a boy during a field trip. A parent in West Virginia told Clearwater reporters that she remembered Parkman sitting in the back of the bus with the boys on a field trip. She spoke bluntly with Clearwater reporters.

"My son went on a trip with Mr. Parkman and brought his camera. When I had the film developed, I saw a picture of Mr. Parkman kissing a boy on the lips, a real kiss. I brought the photo to the District Superintendent who asked the State to investigate. I gave the State a copy of the photo and the next thing I knew, Mr. Parkman moved out of the State to Pottstown, New York." A reporter wrote that West Virginia bureaucrats stopped their investigation when Parkman moved out-of-state.

After growing up in New Jersey, Parkman attended college in West Virginia where he sought opportunities for educational leadership. There he married Linda, who worked as a registered nurse in-between giving birth and raising children who grew up in West Virginia and Pottstown, New York.

Bob's children loved him dearly but often mocked his fastidiousness and teased him about his over-reactions to emergencies. They joked about Parkman carrying expensive cameras in a beer cooler to prevent theft, especially since he was not the beer cooler-type. Teachers joked, too, about his "deer-in-headlights" face whenever he came running into our school after we had called the police or fire department.

The Superintendent's children also loved to tease him about his unwillingness to become more cosmopolitan after moving to Clearwater, less than two hours from New York City. They joked about his choice of restaurants when he'd suggest his favorite lobster or beef chain rather than a more upscale venue. He was not his children's definition of an epicurean.

As I got to know him, it seemed to me that Parkman based most of his decisions on a sincere belief that good wins out over evil; rules keep us safe; people inherently do the right thing; and the constitution and the Bible protect us from evil. He subscribed to a traditional fifties lifestyle, or so it appeared. Parkman had created a community image for himself that was more Mr. Rogers than Mr. T. He seemed so benevolent, kind and trustworthy. Only hindsight shows us how Parkman worked hard to create a public image that masked his real self.

Seth prepared for eighth grade with his own personal School Superintendent. If Parkman had a summer day of meetings, he'd take Seth to a pre-meeting breakfast at a nearby diner. A day off from work for Parkman was an opportunity for more time with Seth.

They shopped for Seth's school clothes and had science lessons in the woods. Shopping sprees and nature walks always included long talks about Seth's family problems. This sometimes annoyed Seth, but he liked the escape from his difficult home-life and stressful neighborhood. "It was very comforting to be with Bob," he testified.

Parkman and I had discussed our own childhoods. We talked about the strained relationships we both had with our fathers. Bob felt that his own struggle for acceptance from his father was the impetus for him to improve Seth's unhappy circumstances.

Those close to the Superintendent could see he fully experienced Seth's fears of entering eighth grade. Parkman saw Seth having the same fears he himself experienced as an adolescent. As such, Seth's fears became Parkman's own fears.

To prevent peer teasing of Seth, Parkman bought him stylish clothing. He took the boy shopping with the permission of Seth's father. However, Dad did not know how extravagant the Super-intendent was with his purchases and was shocked to see a $150 price tag on sneakers that he would have bought in a thrift shop for $3.00. Dad was also unaware of their summer days together be-cause Seth lied about their meetings at Parkman's insistence.

Bob hoped the new clothes would help Seth gain acceptance from other children. He urged Seth not to tell people who had bought the clothes, but Seth very proudly let everybody know the clothes came from Parkman. Seth saw nothing wrong with the gifts.

"I've told him a thousand times not to ever mention me," Park-man yelled in frustration when I once told him Seth continually invoked his name and friendship. Parkman never understood that Seth *needed* to impress people with their relationship after years of being a pariah. Seth was 12 and pride was a new feeling for him, pride derived from his relationship with Parkman. He'd make sure people knew about it despite Parkman's demand for secrecy.

Seth's eighth grade teachers grew suspicious. They saw Park-man rush to the school whenever Seth got in trouble. They were concerned that Seth's need for any emotional supervising would always result in calls to Parkman rather than Seth's Dad. As eighth grade progressed, Seth's oppositional behaviors became more reg-ular, resulting in more regular visits from Parkman. Seth's teach-ers were also upset that he was permitted to use middle school phones to call Parkman.

Middle School staff later testified that Parkman removed Seth from school to "calm him down" whenever Seth misbehaved. Parkman would take him to lunch in a restaurant to restore Seth's mood. Unwittingly, Parkman undermined the Middle School Psy-chologist's efforts to have Seth take responsibility for his classroom behavior. That psychologist, Frank Gaylord, testified that he complained to his district supervisor about Parkman's interference but was ignored. He also testified to leaving anonymous messages about Parkman on the Clearwater Police answering machine.

In eighth grade, Seth felt he had absolute power; he was a friend of the Superintendent. Any adolescent would have felt the same. Some eighth graders get through the day as bullies, while many survive with sports. Other eighth graders take their identity from academic success and there are always a few who enjoy being class clown. For years, Seth was none of these. He had no personal traits that were respected by middle schoolers and he received no positive peer feedback. Suddenly his search for a respected identity was complete. He believed he was Parkman's agent in the Middle School and Bob reinforced this notion.

As the Superintendent's self-appointed middle school representative, Seth complimented teachers, but always sounded supercilious and conniving because his plaudits were inappropriate coming from a child.

"You're doing a great job. I'm going to let the Superintendent know about you," he'd say with great intensity. Seth would later mention the teacher to Bob, whose eagerness to please Seth caused him to provide inappropriate feedback to the teachers.

"Seth tells me you're doing a great job. Keep up the good work."

Everybody enjoys compliments from their boss. So, the complimented teachers would eventually complete this bizarre circle with Seth.

"Thanks for mentioning me to the Superintendent. He came by and shared your compliment." When a teacher completed this circle, Seth felt so powerful that he would lecture the teachers.

34

"It's important to do a good job. When somebody does a good job, they should be acknowledged." His pedantry was offensive, even to the most patient teacher. At 13, Seth could not realize he insulted staff. They eventually grew tired of his pomposity. Although they felt insulted, teachers knew it was Parkman's fault, not Seth's.

After Seth saw his threats and compliments wear thin with teachers, he involved himself with custodians, cafeteria workers and security guards. His adult speech patterns and refined manners made him seem strange as he extended his "power" from the classroom to all corners of his school.

Daily reports of Seth's name-dropping circulated throughout the district. His academic progress and classroom behavior deteriorated because the young boy's personality was being re-structured by his adult friendship and Parkman's power. His teachers felt that Seth totally lost interest in academics and went to school only to serve as Parkman's representative.

At 13, Seth felt omnipotent after a childhood deprived of positive social feedback. He now thought he had more peer-power than the school bully, the school drug dealer, or the prettiest girl. His normal adolescent immaturity kept him from understanding the difference between popularity and notoriety. His circle of friends did not expand as he expected. When Seth tried to impress classmates with a $500 Palm Pilot "gift from the Superintendent," he was surprised to see resentment rather than interest. When he confided to students about his new friend's age and job, they thought it weird rather than enviable. This confused the 13-year old but he continued telling others about his weekends with the Superintendent, which served to further alienate him.

Seth placed the Superintendent on a pedestal and could not understand why other students weren't envious. Seth thought Bob was cool, but even students began to worry. Seth's Middle School teachers unsuccessfully tried to stop the Superintendent from imposing himself on Seth, after which they also reached out to their colleagues at the High School, warning that the High School teachers would soon be seeing their concerns firsthand. They told the teachers about the school departures, the personal gifts and Parkman's emotional over-involvement. The shocked high school teachers shared the news with Nancy Garton, a chairperson also doing an internship with me.

Garton brought this news to me. She also knew I was a friend of Parkman's and might be able to influence him if the teacher gossip was true. I was shocked to hear about this news from the Middle School teachers, especially since I'd been friends with Parkman and he never mentioned Seth.

Our friendship was based on a mutual interest in photography and wildlife. I was lucky enough to have had several recent gallery shows, one in Clearwater. Parkman was a high-level amateur photographer and a true gadget freak. We liked to review photography gadgets and share our latest wildlife photographs. He even went to Cape Kennedy, Florida on overnight wildlife photography workshops. He was a Nikon nut. I had two Nikons.

My prior urban experience and my involvement in photography eventually made me the only principal in Clearwater from whom Parkman would accept personal criticism, even teasingly in front of his family. Our relationship grew to include my family at Parkman family birthdays, holiday parties and barbeques. On several occasions, the Parkmans enjoyed Fourth of July fireworks on my boat as well as other boat trips when their adult children were in town.

On one of those trips which included his wife and two of his four daughters, we went down the Hudson River to the Statue of Liberty and saw Parkman's penchant for over-reaction. The boat engines hit a submerged log in the East River and lost power. We were not in danger of sinking but after I radioed for help, the Coast Guard had to find us and tow us to the Manhattan shore through a very choppy East River. When we were safely docked and calmed with mai tai's, the Superintendent's family teased him about his reaction to the mid-river crisis. He had immediately grabbed a life jacket and his camera-cooler, positioning himself on the stern, ready to abandon ship even before learning our status. A few more mai tai's and they lovingly teased him about a lifetime of similar reactions, giving details and having a grand old time with Dad as the butt of their teasing. He laughed with them.

Parkman's wife, although a nurse and very health-conscious, was always overweight and constantly dieting. She avoided the mai tais. Bob's daughters were slender, vivacious, business-oriented, high-energy types; very mature and worldly for their age, having traveled extensively. I had described these outings to Garton, so she felt I should know about the calls from Seth's Middle School teachers.

Upon learning of the Middle School situation, I called in my Senior Assistant Principal, Tom Nelson, and repeated what I'd just learned. We were dumbstruck. It was hard to believe that a Superintendent who had recently rid our school of several socially problematic staff would engage in similar behavior.

During the prior three years, I had reported two teachers and an administrator to Parkman for having students in their cars or for being with a student in an unauthorized non-school situation. Parkman quickly pressured each to resign or face charges of "conduct unbecoming."

A male teacher had pressured a female student to accept a ride home after a club meeting because a torrential rain began. The student's mom called me to say her daughter declined the ride three times until she felt obligated to accept the ride when the teacher stopped his car next to the girl as she walked home in the rain. Parkman pressured the teacher to resign or face charges.

On another occasion, a parent complained of a male teacher arranging to meet her daughter at a local fast food restaurant after the girl called the teacher from home, saying she wanted to run away. The teacher should have immediately involved our mental health staff but chose, instead, to invite the girl for counseling and a hamburger. Parkman pressured this teacher to resign or face charges.

Months later, one of my male assistant principals took a special interest in a female student. He was seen giving her driving lessons in his car. This administrator was also pressured by Parkman to resign or face charges.

None of the staff I reported to Parkman for extra-curricular fraternizing were adjudicated. They resigned and secured positions in other districts. Were they guilty of anything more than trying to help a student? We'll never know because Parkman convinced them to resign rather than face charges. He convinced them that such charges, whether or not they were guilty, would destroy their careers.

When potential staff misconduct was reported to me, the District Guidelines required me to investigate and provide information to the Superintendent who would interview the individual and provide his findings to the Board of Education President. The Superintendent and Board President were to determine if the case required police involvement.

Once I did my reporting to Parkman on these cases, I had no legal right to know what happened if the staff did not report back to my school. I never knew if Parkman reported these incidents to the police or the State Education Department. From what I knew, it seemed that his entire "investigation" consisted of convincing the accused to resign. The complaining parents were always satisfied. Was Parkman offering these staff the same escape he may have been given in West Virginia?

Assistant Principal Nelson, Garton and I reviewed these cases in light of Parkman's similar behavior with Seth. It was hard to believe the reports from Middle School staff, given the vehemence and disgust Parkman showed over these earlier cases.

I telephoned the Middle School in Nelson's presence for confirmation of the teacher reports.

"Yes, it's true. All this and more," I was told. "Several days ago, during a fire drill when the entire building evacuated, Seth broke from his class and ran to the Superintendent who was observing the drill from his car."

I was surprised at the frustration of some who observed the birth of this relationship and I expressed my own readiness.

"If the Superintendent's behavior isn't stopped while the kid is in middle school, we will do it next year when he's at our school and we will act quickly."

Quite understandably, nobody at the Middle School felt it was their role to give Parkman directives about his behavior with Seth. As Parkman's friend, I felt an advantage and quickly decided not to wait until the boy was our student.

I immediately went to Parkman's office to confront him about what I'd been told.

"I hear a lot of gossip about you having a new friend at the Middle School," I blurted out as I rushed into Parkman's office unannounced.

"What the hell took so long for them to question what I was doing? It's about time they raised concerns. Well, I'm prepared with answers . . . how many times have you or one of your staff mentored a child? Were you questioned?"

Parkman had lots of prepared answers and seemed aware that teachers were already questioning his relationship with Seth.

"Are you taking the boy out of school?"

"Yes."

I reminded him of the staff he pressured to resign.

"I remove Seth with his father's consent and keep your nose out of my business."

In my three years in Clearwater, he had never addressed me in this manner. I chidingly warned him.

"Next year, Seth *is* my business, so watch out. You usually tell me everything. How come you haven't told me about this boy?"

"I haven't told you anything about Seth because I didn't want to hear your criticism. My family keeps giving me crap about Seth and whenever I explain the mentoring, they keep using you as the authority. 'Why don't you ask Mr. Cohen what he thinks about this relationship?'" he whined.

I saw a passion in Parkman I'd never seen before. He stood up at his desk, like a preacher.

"I am lifting Seth out of the gutter and giving him the kind of opportunities his family cannot afford, either financially or emotionally. He has a special ability to understand others. He's brilliant and God has brought us together, brought me to him so I can help him fulfill his potential because American education is not reaching him."

The Superintendent kept returning to a common theme.

"I see a young Bob Parkman in Seth."

Tears came to his eyes as he again told me about his father's military exploits and macho-man approach to life, one that he, himself, could never accept. Parkman sadly again described his father's lack of appreciation for his accomplishments as a teacher, principal, and Superintendent.

"I will nurture Seth the way his own father cannot and my father did not." I left his office very confused and concerned.

This was very disturbing to me. Knowing Parkman's children personally, I felt he should have been quite fulfilled by the job he had done nurturing them. The next day, he unexpectedly came to my office and continued the conversation.

"Even had to buy him new underwear," Parkman proudly told me during this discussion about Seth. He blushed when describing their shopping spree. He was indignant when I shared public perception of their relationship and told me I should be supporting him, as a friend. However, after this first discussion about shopping sprees, computer lessons and walks in the woods with Seth, I had to ask, "Do you feel this friendship is appropriate?"

He then gave me an "official update" about Seth's needs, his family circumstances, his attentiveness to detail and other aspects of Seth's personality.

"Sounds like you're adopting this young man," I teased.

He ignored my comment and as he would many more times, expressed sad concern for the failure of American education to educate "the unusual child such as Seth who would be at the top of his class were he in any European country." He seemed to believe this, ignoring Seth's reality.

Instead, he talked about the boy's "high European manners," seeing them as "courtly etiquette" rather than the pop-androgynous style adopted by many of the Goth-styled students. Until I met Seth, Parkman repeatedly said, "I want you to meet this boy . . . You'll see what I mean . . . he has such wonderful manners."

I avoided meeting Seth because the relationship sounded ill from the onset and I did not want to be seen as supportive. Every time Bob wanted me to meet Seth, I bluntly told him, "Bob, everything I'm hearing from you and the Middle School teachers tells me this is a career-buster. The Middle School teachers think you're in the boy's pants. I'm not meeting him."

"What can you expect from the very same people who don't understand Seth's academic or emotional needs," he responded with a shrug.

"Bob, there are teachers at the Middle School who want to call the police on you. They want you to stop seeing the boy. Leave him alone. This will end your career. Listen to your family and friends!"

Parkman explained his family's position as jealousy. Although I had seen his family tease him, they also loved him dearly, and tried desperately to get him to end his obsession with Seth.

"They don't understand. Nobody understands this boy except me," he cried, tears suddenly rolling from his eyes.

My Superintendent was standing at my conference table crying about a middle school boy I'd not yet met. This did not bode well for Seth, I thought. Since, I'd just learned of the relationship. So, I withheld judgment.

I asked what turned him on about the boy, specifically using that potentially sexual term. Parkman explained he enjoyed the mentoring part most, "filling voids of intellect."

"You're sure that's not the only void you're filling," I interrupted.

He screamed: "Is that what teachers really think, that I'm fucking this kid?"

"People ask why you give him so many gifts if not for sexual favors."

"I'm not ashamed of the gifts."

Throughout that year, Parkman tried to rationalize the relationship to me. He wanted me to take special care of Seth when he entered high school the next year.

"I'm sorry, Bob," I responded. "Just as you told me I should not give your own daughter any special treatment, I will not give Seth any special treatment."

He seemed naïve when I tried to shock him by repeating, "Bob, they believe you are in the boy's pants."

"That's disgusting and I won't tolerate that kind of talk from you or the teachers. Find out who's making such statements about me."

I told him all of Seth's teachers thought of sexual possibilities because he was removing Seth from the building.

"I've only removed him twice and people are acting as if it's a daily thing." Seth later contradicted this in pre-trial testimony.

"It was a regular occurrence for Bob to take me out of school during eighth grade, probably 10 to 12 times in my last few months in middle school."

Seth had bragged to teachers about his weekend breakfasts with the Superintendent. I asked Bob about these reports.

"How did you find that out? I did that only twice. What's the big fucking deal?"

I tried to shock him into some awareness of public perception, but nothing impressed him. He didn't care what people thought. It was frustrating and sad.

The next day, with Mr. Nelson at my side, I telephoned the Clearwater Police Department and spoke with Lieutenant Somerset.

"Have you been hearing any rumors lately about the Superintendent?"

Somerset was coy. "What kind of rumors are you talking about?"

I reviewed my concerns and shared the Superintendent's statements. I repeated the reports from the Middle School teachers. Somerset then told me about the anonymous phone calls, probably from the same middle school teachers.

The Lieutenant was surprised that Parkman admitted removing the boy from school, taking him out for weekend meals, and spending large amounts of money on clothing and other gifts. After hearing about Parkman's admissions, Somerset decided to follow-up on the telephone messages by interviewing Seth's Dad. He asked me to call the Middle School to confirm that Seth was in school that day, after which he and Detective Robinson went to Seth's home. Dad admitted he'd already been concerned about his son's relationship with Parkman. He allowed the police to interview Seth when he came home from school that day.

Seth protected Bob. His dad pleaded with him to tell the truth.

"Is there anything bad going on . . . Does he do anything that makes you scared to tell us what he does?" Seth gave responses he had rehearsed with Bob.

"I have serious issues at home due to my mother's departure, and serious personal problems for which the Superintendent is counseling me. If you want further information, ask Bob."

This routine disclosure from Seth and his advice to "speak with Bob," usually enough to intimidate those who questioned him did not deter Somerset and Robinson. Just before eighth grade ended, they returned to discuss the relationship with Seth's Dad who again expressed deep concern.

"I continuously question Seth about this relationship and feel Seth is honest about the propriety of their activities."

Fears grew that Parkman was abusing the eighth grader. Middle School teachers continued reporting their concerns to any who would listen. They spoke to one of Parkman's Cabinet members who informed Parkman of the teacher's concerns. Parkman then ordered the Middle School to have a staff meeting at which a statement from Parkman was read aloud.

"It has been brought to my attention that a group of teachers at the Middle School are concerned about my mentoring relationship with a student…"

Parkman's emailed statement to the school was later used by the Grand Jury to prove that Middle School staff and administration expressed their concerns about Parkman long before Seth left middle school for Clearwater High School, but nobody listened. And, why should they? Parkman's personality seemed pure and clean.

CHAPTER 7

During April of their eighth grade, all students visit the High School for an orientation, but the Superintendent wanted a private tour for Seth.

"Seth believes he is going to get severely beaten by students at the High School and that someone is going to take his head, shove it into a toilet bowl and drown him."

I asked the Superintendent for his own thoughts about Seth's fears.

"I understand this won't happen, but I'm an adult. He is scared shitless of going into a new school."

Although Parkman knew Seth's fears were unrealistic, he obviously felt the boy's anguish. Parkman was more anxious than most of the over-protective parents who came to my office.

"I really disappointed my father in high school," Parkman again told me. "He wanted me to be like him, the high school hero. But, I had no interest in sports and didn't hang out with those who did." Parkman seemed prepared to do anything to prevent Seth from having the same sad afterthoughts about high school.

On the surface, Parkman had a passion to make Seth successful. I truly believed that Seth's educational needs were motivating the Superintendent to mentor. He seemed emotionally over-involved, but sincere. As I listened to Parkman seriously complain about the failure of schools to educate students like Seth, I had to remind myself that I had already reported him to the police. I had to keep telling myself that Parkman's passion for Seth's academic success could be a cover-up for other passions.

The Superintendent directed me to give Seth a personal tour of the High School and to reassure Seth he'd have a safe harbor with me. I refused.

"I won't do it unless his father comes in or you give me the directive in writing." I knew he would never write it.

He insisted. I rebutted.

My relationship with my boss significantly deteriorated that day because I would not give Seth a tour of the High School. After refusing to give the tour, I called my local union president to let him know I'd been given an inappropriate directive by the Superintendent. My union leaders disagreed with me and told me Parkman's directive was appropriate.

"If the Superintendent feels he is mentoring a child and wants you to see the child individually for crisis intervention, you must do it." I ignored them, too.

The day after I called my union for help, Parkman unexpectedly brought Seth to the High School. Parkman told me that my union president called him and reported my complaint. Nobody could see beyond Parkman's milquetoast personality. They considered any sexual deviance impossible.

I went to the lobby to meet Parkman and Seth after hearing of their arrival on my walkie-talkie. Parkman was starting to fall apart before our eyes. He demanded a special tour for Seth, loudly enough for parents and teachers in the lobby to hear. He then introduced me to Seth who held out his hand in the regal manner Parkman had described.

"I am so pleased to make your acquaintance, Mr. Cohen. The Superintendent speaks so highly of you. I look forward to getting to know you."

My first impression was not of regal manners. These words sounded inappropriate coming from an eighth grader. He also dressed unusually; his dress shirt tucked in and his pants worn too high and tight. He looked like he'd been dressed by an elderly person.

In Seth's presence, Parkman again directed me to give him a tour. I again refused. To prevent an awkward scene in the crowded school lobby, I assigned Holly, a security guard, to give Seth the same tour she'd do for any frightened child.

Holly and Seth left the lobby. I stood near Parkman and watched as Seth peeked into the high school cafeteria holding 600 students. When he saw several tough boys from his neighborhood, he panicked and bolted from the building, taking refuge in the parking lot behind the Superintendent's car.

"Now do you see what I mean," said the Superintendent to anyone who would listen.

Seeing how fragile Seth was, I told Parkman it was now even more inappropriate for Seth to tour without his father present.

"The boy's father is absent as a decision-maker. That's why I must be there for him."

I was reviled by Parkman's "he needs me" speech. The stories we heard about Parkman's interference at the Middle School were now substantiated. This foreshadowed unavoidable tragedy for Parkman and Seth at the High School. I saw that my life was about to change.

Parkman was emotional and flustered. He rushed out to the parking lot, spoke briefly with Seth, and brought him back into the school. I brought them to my office. Parkman glowered at me.

"Could you at least give Seth some advice like you'd do for any other kid!" I agreed to speak with him but only alone. Parkman left my office.

"I don't care whose friend you are. I don't care who you know. When you come to this school, I'm in charge. You will get to class on time, not like in middle school. You will do your schoolwork, not like in middle school. And you will not create scenes. You understand? No phone calls to Parkman from my school and no leaving the building with him unless your father approves. That's the only advice I can give you. If anybody bothers you, go to Assistant Principal Grey. He's your administrator."

I felt terrible speaking to a child in this manner. But, I did not want Seth coming to high school with the same plan he had at middle school. I'd rather have him frightened than under Parkman's control. Seth later testified that he was shocked and confused by my unexpected words of "advice." He expected me to be an "obedient soldier."

My relationship with Parkman deteriorated that day in the lobby. But, I took strength from the teachers who were nearby, witnessing Parkman's pitiful behavior. The teachers immediately voiced their agreement with my actions.

Thus began a battle that became public wherever Parkman thought he could attack my credibility. He knew from the lobby experience that I would defy him regarding Seth.

Parkman began to emotionally deteriorate near the end of Seth's eighth grade, a collapse that would take a year. Colleagues now constantly talked behind his back about the Parkman-Seth relationship. One of his assistants expressed frustration to me about Parkman's emotional state.

"Bern, we spend 50 percent of our time protecting him from himself. He reacts to every complaint by a parent or a teacher as if they were chastising him personally and if we let him react, we'd all be in trouble. Bob feels he can manage everything throughout the district from his computer. He'd be happiest if he never had to speak to another teacher or parent or board member again. He just seems to be falling apart and it could be because of this boy."

Parkman's Assistant Superintendents and staff, along with several school board members, held the District together as Parkman unraveled. They kept the school system functioning for months while Parkman sat idly during the school day, waiting to play with Seth after school.

According to Seth's testimony, it was then, while Seth was still in middle school, that Parkman made a plan to fire me because I would interfere with their relationship when Seth got to high school.

"We have to watch that fat ass Cohen and see how we can fire him. Stay away from him when you get to high school. He wants to split us up. We'll get some people to cooperate and get him fired for intimidating staff and creating a hostile environment."

Seth's sworn testimony included a clear description of Parkman's plan to get me fired, largely dependent on the few teachers to whom I'd given negative evaluations. Parkman's tirades about me were initially private shows for Seth, but they grew to an expanded audience and regularly included his Assistant Superintendents, cabinet members, and union presidents before he started bashing me in public. Parkman knew we'd protect Seth when he entered high school, so he formed a team and a plan against us even before Seth was a freshman.

I foolishly thought my warnings might scare him away from Seth. I also thought I was the only colleague confronting him. His district office staff later testified about their own confrontations with Parkman. He ignored them as he'd ignored me and his family.

CHAPTER 8

After finally having an opportunity to observe Parkman's behavior with Seth, I felt it was necessary to call Seth's Dad before the boy started ninth grade. I told him I had concerns regarding the Superintendent's role with Seth. Dad responded quickly.

"I ask that you keep informing me of any matters regarding my son rather than informing the Superintendent. I wanted that in middle school but Seth insisted on calling Mr. Parkman."

Dad had a very educated vocabulary and thoughtful manner of speech. He did not sound like the "airhead" described by Parkman. I told him our school would call him rather than Parkman if problems arose with Seth. I asked him to meet with me and a counselor to discuss his son's relationship with Parkman. I was soon shocked to learn that Dad immediately informed Parkman of our discussion. The Superintendent had already convinced Dad I was not to be trusted.

Seth's entry into high school coincided with a spike in our school's population resulting from a local economic boom and our school's publicized improvement during my first three years at the helm. Clearwater was at the epicenter of a burgeoning area. Boarded-up mills and strip malls became mega malls. Orange County, New York, less than two hours from Manhattan and on the fringe of rural upstate, had three major intersecting highways connecting to every part of the country.

The interstates and rapid growth of regional shopping brought northeast distribution centers such as ShopRite; major corporate offices, including MetLife; and new students registering at our High School in record numbers. At the County Realtors Conference, local brokers credited the improved high school for the real estate surge. We had reduced school violence so dramatically that it made news in two national education magazines.

In addition to new residents, dozens of private school children re-enrolled in the High School. It was no longer full of "thugs and drugs" as Parkman said when he hired me.

Bob Parkman enjoyed the prospects of being Superintendent of a rapidly growing student population. He spoke at Rotary, Kiwanis, local churches, and other groups who wanted to be part of a future that saw Parkman returning local schools to the glory that was theirs during the Fifties and Sixties. He hated the public speaking but he knew it was part of a Superintendent's survival.

The unexpected surge in population greeting Seth's incoming class resulted in larger classes, overcrowded corridors, scheduling issues and increased discipline concerns. Every Clearwater principal was frantically calling Parkman for additional staff and budget. This huge stress on the Superintendent prevented him from seeing Seth as often as he had been. As such, Seth's instability in his new environment quickly outgrew Parkman's ability to help him. Something was rattling Seth, causing him to constantly lose self-control when he started high school. From the opening day, there were daily Seth-related incidents. His counselors and teachers were immediately concerned. It seemed that something was pre-occupying Seth, causing constant lack of focus and misconduct.

On the third day of high school, Seth told Parkman there was an overall "threatening" nature to the school. His perceptions were real to him but not based in reality. Although the school had become a recognized model of calm, there was always tension around Seth because he created it.

While addressing the most serious, unexpected budget problem of his career, Parkman became so attached to Seth's school day, that he, himself, had constant hysteria and could not handle the budget crisis. Bob and Seth became slaves to each other's emotions.

Within a few weeks, Parkman was calling me daily about "school-wide tension" and fights imagined by Seth. It was quickly apparent that Seth felt he was the Superintendent's investigator at the High School. He was thrilled to be Parkman's informer, usually thinking less about his class work and more about his spying work. He came to school with a purpose, as he later testified: "find things wrong at the High School so I could call Bob and eventually give Bob enough information to fire Cohen."

If there was nothing to report, he would create a ruckus. He felt indispensable, sometimes behaving like a spy in a bad comedy, even wearing a black trench coat that he'd refuse to remove in class. Within his first week at our school, we concluded that Seth contacted Parkman on a regular basis throughout the school day.

We could not figure out how Seth communicated to Bob because we were strict about cell phones and kept an eye on Seth at all times, or so we thought. We later learned that Parkman made arrangements, before Seth even arrived at our school, for Seth to secretly use the phones of two high school staff who were angry because I had given them negative evaluations. Parkman knew who to approach because he had to review all negative staff evaluations.

Seth was so inept at spying, sometimes literally peeking into my office, that he reminded us of Peter Seller's version of Inspector Clouseau.

The 600 students who shared Seth's lunch period, also quickly knew him for outrageous cafeteria disturbances. He would tell his teachers about his fear of being ridiculed by students in the cafeteria, after which he would create a cafeteria disturbance, causing students to taunt him. Seth would be disciplined and brought to an in-school suspension room. Seth would then secretly telephone the Superintendent for assistance, after which Parkman would show up and intervene.

CHAPTER 9

Parkman's daughter, Lynn, was a senior when Seth was a freshman. She and her mom developed steely-eyed concern about Parkman and Seth. Now that Seth was at the High School, Mrs. Parkman and Lynn, independently asked me to speak with the Superintendent about community perception of the relationship.

Lynn approached me in the high school corridor, "Mr. Cohen, when can I see you for a few minutes?"

"Right now," I said. She followed me into my office.

"My father wants me to mentor Seth's sister and I don't want that family in my life." I showed her the note tacked on my bulletin board.

"Take a stand!" signed, "Bob."

"Your dad gave me that shortly after I got to Clearwater." She looked at it and said, "I will."

At a high school event honoring high achievers, Mrs. Parkman whispered to me, "Surprised he didn't want to bring Seth." I told her the truth.

"He *did* want to bring Seth but I wouldn't let him because all the students here are being honored for their academic achievement."

"You're the only one who'll talk to him like that. Why don't you tell him he's obsessed with the boy and it looks bad?"

I thought it would help her to know I'd already challenged him about Seth, but when I explained how I'd confronted her husband, she sighed, "I thought you would be our biggest weapon but he's already withstood you". Although she was frustrated and angry about her husband's public relations naiveté, she did not think they were sexually involved.

When his family reached out to me for help, Parkman was giving them a new, negative opinion of me. He told them, in Seth's presence, that my management skills and popularity had disappeared. Lynn was a very active senior at the school. She knew her father was lying about my popularity. His family also realized that Parkman's new opinion of me was based on my confrontations with him about Seth.

"The parents hate Cohen," Parkman told his family. "They find him crude, rough and distasteful." His family knew otherwise.

Parkman continued calling me about information he received from Seth, always erroneous information.

"You had an emergency at your school and you didn't call me?"

"Could you explain what emergency you think happened," I responded.

"I have information that you called the police today regarding a violent incident at the school and failed to notify me."

"Perhaps, you have been misinformed. Police cars are here because I was meeting with them to implement a drug awareness program, a meeting to which you'd been invited."

Seth was a 14-year old, uninformed ninth grader, but Parkman always believed him. Misinformation from Seth continued until I called Seth into my office.

"I told you when I met you last May that you are to behave like every other student. No other student picks up the telephone to misinform the Superintendent. You are running the risk of being suspended for false reporting if this behavior continues." I explained new Homeland Security Regulations which classified such reporting as a felony.

After school, alone with Bob in his office, Seth repeated every word of my admonishment. Further threats from Parkman came fast. The next day he directed his staff to withhold non-emergency services from the High School. A friend in the Tech Department warned me that calls for assistance from the high school to the District's Technology Department would be ignored. High school staff would then wait weeks for assistance rendered immediately to other schools.

Seth testified that Parkman continued prodding him to "get Cohen."

"Bob told me he convinced several teachers to file charges against Mr. Cohen for stealing petty cash and creating a hostile work environment, but, he wanted me to find more dirt."

Parkman was at war, using any avenue to eliminate what he wrongly thought was the only barrier between him and Seth. I began having witnesses to everything I did or said because Seth was even misreporting my morning public address announcements.

Despite Parkman's constant anger, we managed to have several calm discussions about his need to separate from Seth. He seemed to fade in and out of reality in this regard. We did not know that

Parkman's life, since the middle of Seth's eighth grade, was all about covering-up his sex abuse of Seth. Parkman was now afraid to lose control of Seth, fearing Seth would disclose their sex.

It was exactly this hubris that brought about an emotional collapse. Parkman could not possibly have the mature reality base needed to function in his job as School Superintendent and still have sexual relations with a child. He understood that his friends and family thought the relationship was wrong. He also convinced himself that people totally trusted him and would never learn the truth. His pathology overwhelmed reality and he believed he'd never get caught as long as he controlled the boy.

CHAPTER 10

As Seth's first high school year rolled on, Parkman wondered if he'd still hold Seth's interest or if the high school's diverse sociology would give Seth opportunities to finally be socialized. Parkman shared his ambivalence with me but it now seemed like fear rather than hope.

"I want him to get his own group of friends, but I worry what they'll do to him," adding, he was "worried sick about Seth." Parkman told me he felt too linked to Seth's emotions.

"I want to separate from Seth but I'm unable to do that. I've discussed this with a psychologist." I shared these conversations with the police, hoping to spur them on. I believed Parkman was maintaining the tight relationship with Seth to prevent the now 14-year old from exposing sexual aspects of their relationship.

Parkman's family began questioning his mental state. Although his intellect was accurate about the relationship's "absurdity," as he called it, he continuously expressed a need "to save Seth." No matter how he was threatened by his family or others, he saw Seth daily. He always spoke of Seth's challenges as if they were his own.

He indentified with Seth's fears in a way that made us feel he had fallen in love with Seth.

I challenged the Superintendent to go an entire day without seeing the boy. He accepted the challenge. Parkman kept busy that day by walking throughout District Headquarters, greeting people and starting useless conversation. Finally unable to stay away, he called and told me he was driving around the city, visiting all the schools.

"Cohen, you're next. I'll be at your school in ten minutes."

I immediately called several other principals and learned he'd not visited their schools. He was lying just to get in the door without suspicion.

Parkman arrived at the High School and came directly to my office.

"Where's my friend?"

"Who's your friend?"

"You know who I mean."

"You should try to keep it in your pants once in a while, Bob," I wisecracked, trying to be confrontational but as a buddy. Parkman glared at me. I pointed to the same note I'd shown his daughter.

"How ironic! Now I'm going to take a stand against you unless you tell me you are finished with Seth."

He "directed" me to take him to Seth's classroom. I did that but I refused to leave them alone. Seth later testified, "Mr. Cohen never let us out of his sight when Bob came to see me at the High school. Bob hated that."

"What do you mean by 'never let us out of his sight'? What do you mean by that," the lawyer asked at a pre-trial hearing for Seth's lawsuit against the District.

"I mean when Bob came over to see me at the High School, Mr. Cohen would follow us wherever we went and he never left us alone by ourselves."

"Why do you suppose he did that?" Seth was embarrassed to give the correct response. He avoided the question.

"If we went to the library, Cohen came with us to the library." He gave three other in-school destinations, always adding, "and Mr. Cohen came with us and he always dogged us and acted cold like he was not welcoming Bob, which surprised me because I thought he'd have to be nice to Bob."

When Bob and I were friends, it had been fun greeting him when he visited. Now I greeted him with suspicion and ridicule, whispering into his ear, "I will not be a slave to your emotions," or "Why can't you keep it in your pants." I always hoped he'd crack under the strain and either give up Seth or confess to what we feared.

CHAPTER 11

"Here he is again," Tom Nelson whispered over the walkie-talkie. Senior Assistant Principal Nelson was in charge of the school in my absence. Parkman would always come to the building when I was away. He knew when I was out because principals were required to report our absences to him, even if we left for a brief meeting.

Nelson testified at Grand Jury that Parkman entered the building that day without signing-in, went to Seth's class, and was trying to smuggle Seth out a side door when Nelson "bumped into him" after being tipped-off by security.

"That's not right," Nelson said firmly to Parkman. He shook his head and told Parkman, "You're acting like two kids sneaking out of school." Parkman laughed it off and tried to make the incident funny, but Nelson was angry. He had run across the entire building to intercept the Superintendent just as he was taking Seth out of school without documentation.

"On my watch," Nelson testified, "he was trying to sneak the kid out, and what was he going to do with him?" Nelson was brave to go after Parkman because he did not have tenure at that time and could have been immediately fired by Parkman for insubordination. Tenure's guarantee of due process had not yet been earned by Nelson, who had only been in the position for two years. A muscular former star-athlete from the Clearwater area, Nelson's values would not allow his non-tenured status to prevent him from chastising the Superintendent.

Parkman avoided the security sign-in procedures to prevent documentation of his visits. At a monthly meeting of the Superintendent and the District's principals, I publicly requested that all district staff, including Parkman, sign-in at schools, as do all other visitors. Although I presented several security-related reasons as rationale, Parkman knew I was urging the sign-in so we could monitor him. He approved a new sign-in rule for district staff but ignored it for himself at the High School. Ironically, at the other schools, Parkman would make dramatic entrances, always stopping to chat at the sign-in desk.

Within a few months, it became apparent to our high school teachers that Parkman was behaving in ways for which they'd be fired. We were frustrated, but most of the High School staff were ready to rescue Seth, especially the security team and teachers with whom Seth had regular contact.

"We should set up a better system to document Parkman's arrivals and departures because he knows the building well enough to avoid us," Nelson suggested at my next Cabinet meeting. We devoted that entire meeting to the development of a "Parkman Monitoring System" our "PMS." In addition to Nelson, my Cabinet included two other assistant principals, Steve Grey and Terry Christopher, and Special Education Chairperson, Nancy Garton. She attended our Cabinet meetings because she was completing her administrative internship under my supervision. Our building's security chief, John Norris, was also included in these PMS meetings. Norris was a former sergeant of guards at a high security prison. He was also All-State football linebacker at Clearwater and feared nobody. The few times I had to wrestle a kid to the ground because of a weapon or other circumstances, Norris was always there with me, hands-on.

I started this cabinet meeting by sharing a recent discussion I'd had with Parkman who was enraged because Seth was again being tested.

"He's so intelligent . . . he shouldn't be tested . . . he could teach half the teachers in your school a thing or two."

Bob, you love this kid, don't you," I challenged. Parkman shrugged his shoulders in response. Parkman did not get angry when I said he "loved" Seth. At least he was honest about that.

This Cabinet meeting focused on two issues: how to get Parkman away from Seth and how to document our attempts to stop him.

"How bizarre. Our goal for this meeting is to stop our Superintendent from socializing with one of our students? Hello, anybody home? Nobody believes us out there!"

"I feel like I'm in a movie but I know I'm in your office," Christopher said.

"Too bad it's real," Nelson added.

I pointed out that we were still responsible for Seth, even if he rejects our attempts to help him.

"I want you to know I reported my concerns to the police last Spring when Seth was still at the Middle School. Seth's Middle

School teachers told several of our teachers about Parkman. The police have known about this for a year. We should continue talking to the police but we should also try to stop Parkman. Eventually, if he's guilty and caught, we'll want to show what we did to stop him." I reviewed my recent action.

"This morning, I made another report to the police. If he continues to take Seth out of the building, I will also involve school board members because the police said they cannot prevent Parkman from removing Seth from school if Dad approves. And, nobody knows of any actual criminal behavior on his part."

I told my Cabinet the police wanted us to make no written reports because Parkman would learn about the reports and avoid getting caught. The blackout on reports did not preclude my verbal reports to District leadership.

To me, the best course of action was anything that might save Seth, whether it was the police, us, or the District. Since the police were not making progress due to Seth's lack of disclosure, I felt a need to expand our reporting.

I interacted with Lieutenant Somerset almost daily about normal high school occurrences: a fight, a robbery, or other things that happen when you have 2,000 teenagers in one building. I would also regularly share with him our latest observations of the Superintendent's behavior, especially if he took Seth out of the building. Somerset always asked, "Did you see anything criminal?" As much as I wanted to indict Parkman for removing Seth from school, we never saw any inappropriate physical contact.

"The most physical contact I've seen was Parkman touching the kid's back in the corridor after removing him from in-school suspension," I told Somerset.

At this Cabinet meeting, we designed monitoring procedures and codes to document Parkman's arrivals and departures at our school. When we started the documenting, Bobby Rodriguez, our front door security guard, reported that Parkman always avoided the sign-in process by ignoring the front desk.

"Sign in for him, Bobby, if he doesn't want to sign in for himself so we keep a record of his visits," Norris directed.

After that, Rodriguez always greeted the Superintendent with a hearty "Good Morning" or "Good Afternoon," held up the sign-in book for his signature, and signed in for him when he ignored the book which happened on most of his visits. At Grand Jury, I was required to detail nearly a hundred sign-ins we did for Parkman.

Students were permitted to leave school during the school day only if a parent, guardian or other authorized adult visited the school's attendance office to complete a sign-out request form. The adults were also required to sign-out at the front door where they had initially entered.

If I was not present in the lobby for the Superintendent's arrival, he would ignore the sign-in process. In an attempt to force Parkman's use of security procedures, we used code words over the walkie-talkies to indicate his approach to the building, after which Norris and I would race to the lobby. The first warning of his arrival usually came from Biggie, a security guard posted outside in the parking area or from Wizard, a second-floor guard, sighting him from a window. I'd hear the signal and rush to the lobby with Norris. Only on those occasions, would Parkman sign in.

"He must think we spend a lot of time in the lobby," joked Norris. "He's so screwed-up that he doesn't realize we always try to meet him here." Norris often made me laugh in tough situations. We knew Parkman could listen to our walkie-talkie chatter on his own scanner, so, we constantly changed the code words for his approach.

By winter, the Superintendent was "mentoring" Seth at our school two or three times a week, removing him from school weekly.

"You cannot take this child out of school without parental permission," I said, confronting him on one occasion at the front door. "This is wrong."

"I am the Superintendent and I can do what I think is right. His father is aware I take him from school for counseling. You have no idea what this boy is going through and I have no reason to share it with you. I will remove this child for mental health reasons when and if I see fit." He yelled loudly, with Seth at his side. Unfortunately, Parkman had convinced Seth's dad to continue listing him as a legal sign-out for Seth.

Although we were in a very public place, a lobby large enough to hold 200, I was not afraid of Parkman's raised voice or threats. His screams rebounded off the marble walls and only made me and others in the lobby more aware of his irrationality. He did not care that his self-defense was heard by staff and passing students. He was desperate to be perceived as righteous.

At this point, it didn't matter if Parkman was in love or was evil. His public irrationality showed us he had no boundaries and could be guilty of anything. It had to stop. We had to increase our efforts.

Operating for worse-case scenarios, Norris made copies of the lobby sign-in book on a daily basis and hid them should Parkman steal the book. We worked like detectives because nobody else could find the truth or stop the obsession. The real detectives were at a loss because of Seth's denials.

CHAPTER 12

I asked Dr. Guevara, the school psychologist, to get involved with Seth. Guevara was concerned and got Dad's permission to meet with Seth regularly. He questioned Seth about Parkman at their sessions, but Seth stuck to the "mentoring and counseling" story that Parkman and he rehearsed. Guevara persisted. He was not convinced about mentoring because Parkman and the boy were both showing unusual behaviors.

Seth complained to Parkman about Guevara's pressure to discuss their relationship. Parkman immediately called me with threats to Guevara's future in Clearwater. He wanted Guevara out of Seth's life because Guevara was on-target.

"If Parkman is not abusing Seth, he will be soon," Guevara said repeatedly.

Parkman grew extremely wary of Guevara. He called me daily for a week, giving me a list of violations he wanted to throw at the psychologist.

Dr. Guevara, an athletic type who coached track after school, did not have much contact with me prior to Seth's arrival. We had been "soldiers" in the cultural revolution of the Sixties and

Seventies but on different coasts. I got my "revolutionary" experience in the civil rights and student movements of the Northeast. Guevara, from Los Angeles, was a student activist at Berkeley.

Parkman directed me to ask Guevara to keep a log describing his student contacts. However, Guevara was committed to a free-flowing relationship with his clientele, and did not maintain traditional logs. He worked only with the most stressed-out kids and was often more successful counseling them in the café or the gym.

Parkman's hostility brought me and Guevara together with common causes – the protection of Seth, and ourselves. We quickly developed a mutual respect for what each could do to expose the Superintendent's behavior, and became close confidants and fellow activists in the rescue of Seth. We met daily to plan our on-going intervention of Parkman. Although I had the more radical ties experience, Guevara was now more radical as he became more frustrated with Seth's difficulties. He was convinced that Seth's constantly disruptive behavior was due to sexual abuse.

Just before Thanksgiving of Seth's ninth grade, Guevara was especially aggravated about Parkman. "You need to look Parkman in the eye and say, 'You're fucking this kid, aren't you.'" I took his advice but applied it with more tact.

We knew our careers were at stake if we continued a drawn-out battle against our boss. As the boy's psychologist, Guevara asked for assistance from his District Coordinator, Vera Lewis. Unfortunately, she totally disagreed with Guevara about Parkman's obsession. She even stymied our attempts to stop Parkman. Instead of helping us protect the child from Parkman, she continuously defended him. "He would never harm a child," she said. From her perspective, she was correct, like everybody else she fell for the Jekyll-Hyde ruse. When others asked her about the much-gossiped relationship, Lewis publicly blamed me for Parkman's over-involvement with Seth. She told Guevara and others that I was "continuously singling out Seth for severe and unusual discipline, causing Seth to call the Superintendent for help."

Unable to stop Parkman by having Guevara badger Seth or by publicly confronting Parkman with anger, I called another Cabinet meeting and, for the third time that month, I pointed to Parkman's note on my bulletin board.

"It's time to take a stand."

We faced a problem experienced by no other high school administrators in America. We were convinced our Superintendent was behaving inappropriately with our student, even though we had seen no sexual misconduct.

"We must bring our concerns to a wider overview. In case I die tonight," I told my Cabinet. "I want you to know I am going to my supervisor to share our concerns."

We reviewed the District Guidelines for reporting possible sexual misconduct by staff. The guidelines required a principal to report such concerns to the Superintendent. The Superintendent must investigate the concerns and report his findings to the School Board President. I had already reported to the Superintendent, to no avail, so I was doing the next best thing, reporting to his assistant who also was my direct supervisor. Had I been able to see the future, I'd have worn a tape recorder from that moment on because, no matter where we went for help, Parkman's Jekyll-Hyde persona made us look foolish.

Worried about Parkman's growing paranoia, I disguised my reason for being at my supervisor's office by first visiting Parkman.

We talked about photography and local politics until I knew he'd consider it a "visit." I then went to Ross' office.

"We need to talk about Bob's relationship with Seth. That's why I'm here. We need to do something because who knows what's really going on?"

Ross grunted, grimaced, stood up and locked the door. "I lock it because Parkman walks in here without knocking when he gets paranoid about people visiting me."

I told him how Parkman was now coming to see Seth two or three times a week and how I had confronted Parkman. I also explained how we were monitoring his visits to Seth.

"What can we do," he exclaimed, "he's the Superintendent."

My heart sank. I had hoped Ross could do something to stop Parkman. He was a strength in Parkman's Cabinet and I thought he could rally others to confront him. I cut the meeting short when he again spoke of the Superintendent's "ultimate power." Even Ross felt helpless in a system designed with so much power at the very top. Although he felt powerless, Ross did not think there was any sex involved.

I called Lieutenant Somerset, described my meeting with Ross and told him I was planning to bring our concerns to Dr. Fletcher, the School Board President.

I called my Cabinet together again.

"If I die tonight, I want you to know I'm visiting Dr. Fletcher's office on my way home from work. I'm going to give him this memo documenting our observations of Parkman's behavior."

Fletcher was a successful optician. Knowing his reputation for detail, I prepared a comprehensive memo. I distributed copies for the Cabinet to read, after which I collected and shredded all but two. Board members were elected politicians, which meant I was entering a world of mistrust. I knew it was the right thing to do, but it felt like I was diving into a pool of piranhas by going to Fletcher.

I told his receptionist, "I need to see Dr. Fletcher regarding an emergency." The receptionist disappeared into a maze of examining rooms and returned to say, "Dr. Fletcher will see you shortly."

I sat in the waiting room, surrounded by patients. Dr. Fletcher, tall and thin with the latest fashionable doctor-wear and sporting a pony tail, appeared and waved me into an examining room.

"Well, what brings you to see the optician?"

"I'm not sure you know the town is buzzing about the Superintendent's long-standing, possibly inappropriate relationship with a boy."

"Heard something, but not specific," he answered, evasively.

I described Parkman's visits to Seth. I also told Fletcher I was documenting conversations I'd had with Parkman.

"Mr. Cohen, do you think Mr. Parkman is having a sexual relationship with the boy?"

"I have no such knowledge, but he's acting so weird it makes one wonder. This memo documents our observations. Please read the memo so we can discuss it."

Dr. Fletcher took the memo, thanked me, and told me he'd call if he had any concerns after reading the memo.

"With all due respect, sir, I need to sit here while you read it. That's how important it is. I need to tell the High School teachers that I know you are aware of our concerns and you are ready to take action, or they will go public with their concerns."

Dr. Fletcher looked at me with raised eyebrows. I thought he might direct me to leave. He was my ultimate superior.

"I have no options, Dr. Fletcher. When you read this memo, you'll understand."

Fletcher leaned against a desk and started reading. He kept shaking his head. "If this is true, what a disaster for the District," he said after reading the first page.

The optician's body sank onto a stool as he continued to read. Each page of the lengthy memo resulted in two or more "tsks," and each page turn was accompanied by a woeful headshake or a pitiful "no." Several times during his reading, Fletcher glanced up wide-eyed at me.

"This is terrible," he said when he finished reading. I took it back from him, explaining I had to fax it to my lawyer to ensure it contained no libel or slander.

"What do you want me to do," asked Fletcher. I reviewed the reporting guidelines, and told him I'd already "spoken with" Parkman. I did not tell him I'd already reported to the police.

I suggested he stop the Superintendent from seeing Seth by giving him a cease-and-desist letter from the Board. I also asked him to report to the police. He agreed to take my requests to the school district's lawyer, Kevin Miller.

CHAPTER 13

I knew I risked my career by reporting such concerns to Fletcher without any proof. I also knew the rumors in town were rampant enough to have reached Fletcher prior to my visit. Hearing from me that Parkman was sneaking Seth out of school for hours, would prompt Fletcher to act.

Fletcher then discussed his own relationship with Parkman. He told me his recent meetings with Parkman never focused on education issues because Parkman needed so much emotional support.

"I did not realize that Parkman's emotional demise was linked to the rumors. I thought he was just depressed."

Anybody who knew Parkman did not give the rumors any credibility. The stories they heard did not fit the Parkman they knew. Anyone like Fletcher who knew about Parkman's overall commitment to improving education and his devotion to family and faith, could not consider Parkman a pedophile.

During the prior year, Parkman and Fletcher each had told me they did not trust the other. Now, I was certain neither of them would trust me. Parkman had said, in a very negative tone, that Fletcher was gay. "Fletcher's haircuts and wardrobe are too feminine," he'd say. He often pointed out potential "gay indicators" in people. He did this so often and about so many people, that, prior to my learning of his involvement with Seth, I thought he was homophobic.

Fletcher went on to tell me he thought Parkman was a "weak leader, poor decision-maker, and lackluster cheerleader."

"His heart is in the right place and he cares about kids. But, I'm embarrassed by his personal weaknesses and childish antics, especially during televised Board meetings."

He saw an immaturity in Parkman, but did not think he could be a pedophile. Fletcher promised me "quick action." When I asked what that meant, he only then admitted to hearing the rumors and surprised me by sharing that he and his Vice President, Theresa Bradley, already had a two-hour meeting with Parkman about his relationship with Seth. I was stunned. I thought my staff and I were the only people trying to separate Parkman from Seth while, in fact, the highest authorities in the District were doing the same. After Fletcher described how they "chastised him regarding the rumors," I asked how Parkman responded to their meeting.

"He was very defensive, insisting he was only mentoring the boy. It took two hours for us to discuss public perception because he gave the public no credibility. We told him to remove himself from the boy's life."

Parkman later confirmed this meeting.

"I was very insulted by Fletcher and Bradley's rude demands based only on public perception rather than fact," he whined in the privacy of my office.

Dr. Fletcher and Ms. Bradley had confronted Parkman after hearing the rumors. They also gave him a written warning and believed his promise to separate from Seth.

"So, Dr. Fletcher, what will you do now that I'm telling you he ignored your letter by seeing the boy many times since," I asked.

"I'll speak with our school lawyer and I'll take immediate action. He'll lose his job if he continues to see Seth."

During the weeks following my meeting with Fletcher, I saw no change in Parkman's behavior. He still ignored security regulations. He continued to remove Seth from school.

Parkman complained vehemently when I stayed with him during his visits to Seth. I told him I was chaperoning his visits so I could defend him against the rumors. "If I'm witnessing your meetings with Seth, I can vouch that nothing bad happens." I didn't care if Parkman believed me. It was the only way to protect Seth when Parkman visited.

CHAPTER 14

After Fletcher read my memo, I called our union's lawyer to protect myself. "I find this hard to believe," said the lawyer, Leo Bush, after I described our situation.

"Are you and Parkman getting along . . . does this have to do with some issue you might have with him . . . I don't believe a Superintendent would give up his entire career for a 14-year-old boy. Don't tell anyone that you put something in writing. This can be really damaging for you if you're wrong. Never put stuff like this in writing," Bush advised, again.

I told Bush I'd gone to the police over a year earlier after confirming reports of the Superintendent's behavior at the Middle School. I also told him I had taken my concerns to supervisors and shared them with my Cabinet.

"The whole school thinks he could be in the boy's pants," I explained.

"Did you document his visits?"

"Of course. I documented his visits because I don't expect anybody outside our school to believe us, just like you don't." I could sense that Bush was listening but was frightened by the possibilities. He wanted nothing to do with this.

When I told him I already had shared a descriptive memo with the School Board President, he moaned.

"You went to the School Board President?"

I faxed the memo to Bush. We agreed to speak the next day.

Before speaking again with Bush, I re-visited my supervisor hoping to incite some participation. After five minutes of hearing my description about Parkman's recent behavior, Ross invited another supervisor into the room.

"We spend half our time protecting him from himself," they both whispered. I raised the specter of sexual possibilities.

"You only see the half of it," they agreed. "You only see when Bob goes to your building to be with the boy. How often is that? A couple times a week? You don't see Seth like we see him. He comes here almost every day after school to play with his friend, Bob." They both had confronted Parkman about Seth and later testified about Seth's visits to Bob.

"Seth comes in here every day like he owns the place, never signing in. He greets every secretary and administrator as if he were the Superintendent entering the building."

Seth always tried to engage the adults around him. Just a child, he never knew how intrusive he was with his effusive greetings. His mature vocabulary and veneer of maturity was a defensive style. Inside, he was a socially immature adolescent.

Under oath, Seth testified he went to Parkman's office dozens of times and was given confidential information about teachers, contract negotiations, staff salaries and other data to which only the Superintendent and personnel director had access. Parkman had convinced Seth that district office staff were his friends and high school administrators were his enemies.

Our strict discipline and disregard for Parkman's power was a puzzle to the 14-year old. My three Assistant Principals were staunch in denying Parkman's intervention into their discipline. Once, Parkman snuck into the High School and brought Seth to Assistant Principal Christopher so Seth could apologize for his misbehavior. Christopher did not allow Parkman to have his way.

She had assigned Seth detention after a series of outbursts including a defiance of her. After 30 years experience as a teacher, guidance counselor and administrator, Christopher had no compunctions about assigning the Superintendent's friend to detention. However, Seth felt he should not serve the punishment and convinced Parkman to plead his case.

"I'm not here to ask you to ignore Seth's behavior. I am here because he owes you an apology and I want him to do that," Parkman said without even saying "hello."

Christopher explained that apologies were not enough. "A change in behavior would be best." Parkman was struggling to be the sole arbiter over Seth's behavior.

"That may be so, but I insist he apologize."

Christopher made certain that Parkman understood that apologies would not eliminate detention. They were surprised by her recalcitrance. She stood strong before her boss, controlling her anger at his breach of protocol. She listened while Seth apologized.

"I am very sorry for my behavior. I have serious problems at home. I need to learn to cope with those problems and not have them result in bad behavior at school. Again, I apologize for my behavior. If you have any questions, please ask the Superintendent."

Parkman left. Christopher sent Seth to class and ran to my office in a rage about the Superintendent's attempt to usurp her role as Seth's disciplinarian.

"How dare he bring Seth to me for an apology, thinking I'd let him out of his detention."

My administrators' time was often monopolized by Seth's misconduct. We waited for Parkman's intervention when Seth's behavior would lead to consequences.

I questioned Seth weekly about his relationship with Parkman. Guevara and several teachers did the same. In one of our meetings, Seth told me he was "working" for the Superintendent as his office messenger after school. Parkman was using Seth as an office courier, hoping staff would learn to like him. In so doing, Parkman fed further into Seth's insecurities because the teen felt awkward going into people's offices. This discomfort made him act and speak more pretentiously, creating a vicious circle that ended with the adults thinking he was obnoxious.

On one occasion, Parkman asked Seth to bring an envelope to Ross. He walked right by Ross' secretary, handed the envelope to the second highest person in the District and said, "Hi, Donald. Bob asked me to give you this." A former collegiate basketball player at 6'4", as well as a former marine, "Donald" stood ramrod upright at his desk and looked down at Seth.

"Young man, don't you ever call me 'Donald' again. You may call your friend, Mr. Parkman, by his first name, and that's between you and him. But between you and me that would be the last time you refer to me by my first name. Get it?"

Seth got the message but was not bothered, having been ordained as untouchable. He kowtowed gratuitously.

"I will never address you by your first name again, Mr. Ross. I am very sorry that I offended you. If…"

"Enough!" Ross interrupted.

Through no fault of Seth's and due entirely to the misguided "mentoring," the 14-year old aggravated most of the district office staff. Parkman continued pushing Seth into awkward situations, trying to improve his self-image. Parkman also continuously validated himself to Seth.

"No school system could meet your intellectual needs and you're fortunate, as such a bright student, to have a mentor who is Superintendent."

Seth lived in two worlds, both bizarre. He had the manipulated "puppeteer" world of Parkman controlling every aspect of his life lest he disclose the sordid elements of their "mentoring." Seth's other world included poverty, a relocated mother, and a single-parent father responsible for three children.

When Parkman took more control of Seth, bringing him into an unreal world, Dr. Guevara and Seth's High School teachers were the only positive constants in his life. They gave him a daily dose of reality. Guevara helped the teachers implement classroom procedures aimed at preventing Seth's misconducts, basically keeping him very busy and constantly focused. When the classroom controls were effective, Seth moved his disruptions to the common areas such as corridors and the cafeteria.

Dr. Guevara's counseling was aimed at creating a sense of reality about Seth's friendship with Parkman. But, that reality never took hold because Seth would tell Parkman about his counseling sessions, allowing Parkman to undo Guevara's work. Parkman convinced Seth that Guevara "is an extension of Cohen who's trying to take my (Parkman's) job." This resulted in even more serious disruptions by Seth.

Seth's misbehavior in the cafeteria, a 600-seat "pressure-cooker" of a room, would result in disciplinary consequences which always set up a rescue from Parkman. One of Seth's disruptions, in hindsight, was Seth's expression of Parkman's control over him.

"I own you, I own your mind, your brain is under my power, you will do what I want...," Seth said, while standing unseen behind a seated student. Other students saw Seth waving his fingers over the student's head like a hypnotist while making his weird proclamation.

"Get the fuck away from me you fuckin' weirdo," the student said, but Seth continued the strange, slow incantation.

"You cannot order me to do anything. You will obey my commands because I own your mind."

The student stood quickly, causing Seth's hands to touch the student's head.

"You fuckin' hit me," the student said as he grabbed Seth. Security and lunch-duty teachers immediately separated them and brought them to an administrator. Parkman showed up on cue. This exact scenario occurred three times. Seth would disrupt a 600-student cafeteria, almost starting a riot, and Parkman would immediately arrive to rescue him from discipline.

The over-crowded cafeteria had 58 tables of students eating from disposable cardboard trays and plastic plates and bowls. The noise of 600 teens was amplified by cinder-block and tile walls. On a normal day, it was difficult to hear fire drill bells in that airplane-hanger sized room. Public address announcements never penetrated the din. In this environment, student tension could rise quickly and a student fight could result in a riot.

After Seth's third dangerous café incident, we arranged for him to have lunch in an office, away from other students. There would be no more chanting behind a seated student while dozens of other students cheered for a fight.

Parkman refused to understand that Seth was falling apart under the pressure of their relationship. The Superintendent expected Seth to function normally in school while he was being sexually molested out-of-school.

In picking targets for his "brain-owning" chant, Seth always selected the school's toughest kids because he knew he'd get a rise out of them. And, he'd always select a student sitting close to a security guard so he'd never actually get hit. Although security would intervene before punches were thrown, a near-riot of hundreds was always on the brink whenever Seth would go after a "victim." The riot was his real goal, serving Parkman by forcing the school to appear out-of-control. We had figured out his purpose but did not realize Seth's oft-repeated chant had such significance to his relationship with Parkman.

"I own your mind….you will do as I want…"

Seth's realistic time with teachers and Dr. Guevara were always followed by unrealistic hours with Parkman. This daily emotional roller coaster was thrust upon a boy already confronting a myriad of issues.

His teachers and Dr. Guevara were strict with Seth. Although we believed his behavioral problems were caused by constant internal struggle about his relationship with Parkman, teachers were told to maintain a strict discipline policy. Seth needed to have something realistic in his life even if it was nothing more than organized classroom procedures.

Guevara relentlessly questioned Seth about the Superintendent's behavior. He tried to push Seth to disclose what he felt was certain, but Seth continuously defended Parkman and lied about their sexual relationship. Guevara based his certainty on the continuous emotional displays, Parkman's and Seth's.

Seth knew we questioned him because of Parkman's presence at our school. Yet, he continued disrupting classes and calling Parkman when he was punished, reinforcing their relationship for all to see. Disruption was followed by punishment; followed by Parkman's intervention attempts; followed by our severe questioning of Seth. The boy knew the disruptions would bring our questions. He may have subconsciously been disruptive in order that we continue the questioning, reaching out to us for rescue but afraid to disclose.

Teachers learned to quickly intercept Seth's daily disruptions. They did not allow him to dominate their classes. They removed him from class at the slightest outburst, knowing they'd have to face the Superintendent. They were brave.

CHAPTER 15

As Seth's ninth grade progressed, pressure on Parkman was mounting at home. Lynn was witnessing her father's frequent visits to our school to see Seth. She brought the gossip home and confronted her father. Arguments ensued.

Parkman grew reluctant to bring Seth home on weekends because the family was outright belligerent. He came to my office and accused me of turning his family against him. I couldn't understand why he told me his family confronted him about Seth, not after what I'd already said about Seth. The Superintendent was losing his grip on reality.

With Lynn often reporting to Mom that Parkman visited Seth at school, the family took a stand and refused to allow Seth in their home. They also made Parkman choose between Seth and them for family activities. Parkman always chose family because he could bring Seth to his home when Linda was at work and Lynn was in school. The house was very available despite family protestations. Visits to Parkman's home gave the Superintendent opportunities for child molestation in his own house, in his own bed.

Parkman had still enough of a reality base to know his actions were illegal. Still, the 54-year-old School Superintendent, loving husband and devoted father, took major risks with a young boy's life. Handshakes became hugs and sexual fantasies became sex crimes.

With his home now off-limits when family was there, Parkman began meeting Seth at various locations out-of-town. Dr. Guevara spotted them at a distant town diner having lunch with a school board member. Parkman often tried to legitimize the relationship by including other authority figures for part of their jaunt. Several times, he invited me to an off-campus lunch with Seth. I'd always anger him by telling him, "I refuse to be seen with the two of you."

Always chubby, Bob was now dieting and noticeably slimmer. People quietly whispered that Parkman's diet was an attempt to be more appealing to the slender Seth. He successfully reduced his ample paunch by 30 pounds with a diet "for rabbits only," as he called it.

"With whom are you having an affair," I teased. He gave me a quizzical look. I told him, "such a dramatic weight loss could only be for a lover." Of course, I feared that his lover was Seth because he spoke of little else.

The Superintendent was gushingly proud of his slimmer look. If he wasn't talking about Seth, he was discussing his diet. One day, excited about his new clothes, he threw open the door to my office while I was discussing Parkman-Seth with Guevara and Garton. He was wearing tight jeans and a t-shirt. After our initial shock at his sudden appearance, he proclaimed, "Don't I look buff?" The three of us looked at him and then at each other, not knowing how to respond. I finally answered, "Yeah, you look great."

Parkman seemed confused. He looked like he was thinking, "How could a principal, a psychologist, and an intern, blow me off like this?" He turned and left without a word.

The next day, in an officious manner and a dark suit, he returned to my office.

"Do I look more like your vision of how a Superintendent dresses? You're a lot more traditional than you'd like people to think you are." He was upset that we had not fawned over his weight loss and stylish casual look.

Seth's days in school became more stressed. Parkman would unexplainably learn of Seth's moods, even when there was no incident, and come to the High School to calm him and give him reassurance.

On one of those visits, we had another screaming battle at the front door.

"You cannot do this to us . . . You are undermining whatever progress we make with Seth . . . Every time we help him take a step forward in his development, you come over and put him back two steps."

"You're not a psychologist," he yelled.

"Tell me who knows more about kids' development you or me? You with your degree in teaching Spanish or me with my degrees in Psychology?"

"I know him better than anyone in the world," he countered. "I know Seth better than his parents know him." It was frightening to hear this because he seemed to believe it.

On another of his visits to our school, Parkman got past our entry monitoring and took Seth to the attendance office to sign him out. Norris saw them and ran to my office. We confronted him at the front door.

"Hey, what's up? Where you guys going?"

"I'm just gonna take him for a quick lunch and we'll be back."

Parkman lied saying that Seth was "feeling distraught because of things happening at home. He needs time out from school."

"You think that's a good idea? How about letting him spend some time with his school psychologist if he's upset?"

"I know what I'm doing. Step aside."

The Superintendent took Seth from school and drove home to an empty house. Lynn was at school and Linda was at work. Bob and Seth were alone. To my surprise, Parkman later described a sexual conversation he'd had that day with Seth.

Parkman told me he asked Seth, "Can we talk about your social development? Have you had any dating experiences? I think your messed-up parents had a negative effect on your social development and you have some catching up to do."

"What are you talking about, Bob."

"I'm talking about dating, going out with girls, having sexual experiences with girls."

Parkman probed and further wove the conversation with Seth into a discussion about his own sexual development.

From the taped phone conversations and from Seth's own testimony, it is clear that Parkman guided the boy's words to make Seth ask for sex. He also tried to convince Seth their sex was not gay.

"What we are discussing is okay because most males have their first sexual discussions and masturbation experiences with other males. It's not gay. It's male bonding. This is not gay as long as it is true friendship, rather than romance," Parkman told him, according to the boy's testimony.

Seth always felt trapped between pleasing his powerful friend and finding ways to avoid the sex. It was a difficult time for the already-stressed Seth who was lured by a "bait and switch" sale of lifestyles. Parkman offered a bright alternative to Seth's personal difficulties but substituted a destructive stress: sex. He made Seth his lover while Seth thought he was being groomed to be an adoptive son.

I asked Parkman if he ever thought of legally adopting Seth.

"That thought actually crossed my mind when I saw how similar we are, more similar than I am with my own children."

If Parkman truly thought of Seth as a son he was creating, he was extremely narcissistic in trying to create Seth in his own image. If he actually felt like the "surrogate father" he described himself to be, his crime went beyond child molestation into the absolute worst taboo, incest, in a figurative sense.

One day, we were astounded that Parkman came to the school only minutes after Seth was assigned in-school suspension for causing a disruption. Only after Parkman's arrest did Seth's testimony expose two High School staff who had direct orders from Parkman to allow Seth use of their phones. They also called Parkman if Seth needed him and couldn't get to a phone. They were counselors to whom I had given negative evaluations. Their rebellion against me facilitated further abuse of Seth.

Parkman left the school after calming Seth. I supervised his visit, then returned to my office. But, the Superintendent quickly returned to the building on the pretense of having forgotten something. After avoiding me, he retrieved Seth from the suspension room and snuck out a kitchen door, the only exit beyond the reach of security cameras. He was familiar with our security plan.

Parkman took Seth for lunch in a restaurant. A young boy from a poor family was easily impressed by anything that wasn't fast food. After lunch, Parkman called his office to cover his absence, telling his secretary he was making unannounced visits to schools. He invited Seth to his home for more computer talk.

In the living room, the Superintendent handed Seth a new lap-top and sat next to him on the sofa. Seth testified that Parkman put his hand on the lap-top to balance it on Seth's knees but slowly moved his hand under the lap-top to rub the boy's thighs. Seth ignored this and tried to focus on the computer screen but Parkman explained his actions: "There's nothing wrong with making you feel good. This is not about being gay. It's about two people caring for each other. What we do is not gay. The fact that we're both male," he explained, "doesn't matter because I'm not gay. I love my wife and children."

The 14-year old later told his attorney that he was confused by the Superintendent's use of the "not gay" rationale to approve their sex. When this got stale, Parkman always reminded Seth of all he had done to care for him and his family: the gifts, school clothes, restaurants, their companionship, and his constant intervention into Seth's school matters. Seth would feel guilty and allow Parkman to further destroy his adolescence.

That day, Parkman did not "smuggle" Seth back into school. Instead, he brazenly drove to the front door and dropped Seth off to walk alone from the car and enter school in an extremely hyper state. Within minutes, Seth lost control and misbehaved in his next class.

As usual, Seth was brought to his administrator, Ms. Christopher.

"What's up with you today, Seth . . . You were acting so bad this morning that teachers assigned in-school suspension for a time out . . . Then Parkman came and removed you from school to calm you down . . . now you're more hyper than you were this morning?"

"I have serious problems at home. Mr. Parkman is counseling me regarding these problems. If you have any further interest in these problems, you must contact Mr. Parkman." Christopher sternly explained she was not concerned about his home, "only about your behavior in school."

"The Superintendent would not be happy with you," Seth responded.

"Stop immediately," she yelled. "Don't you ever threaten me again by using your relationship with the Superintendent."

Seth often invoked the Superintendent's name to prevent disciplinary action but Christopher was not intimidated. That was not her style or the style of any CHS administrators. This confused Seth.

Seth reported angrily to Parkman that he heard a High School teacher ridicule him. He was shocked when that teacher told the Superintendent, "Don't come into my classroom, Mr. Parkman, the way you went into Seth's classes at the Middle School." This resistance further confounded Seth's already-confused perceptions.

Christopher kept Seth in her office for administrative detention. He was stressed from what later we learned was sexual time with Parkman. Christopher kept him busy with clerical tasks for two hours until he was calm.

I called Seth's father again.

"I need you to come into school again to clarify your awareness and approval of the relationship between your son and the School Superintendent, and I want to know, in writing, the reasons you give permission for your son to leave school with Mr. Parkman."

One year later, Seth asked his father to leave the room while he testified about his sexual experiences with Parkman. Seth felt guilty about being sexually manipulated and also about having continuously lied to his father. Dad left the deposition room to give Seth freedom to speak about Parkman.

All eyes followed Dad as he embarrassedly skulked out of the room. Although Seth had repeatedly lied, Dad felt he'd been irresponsible in ignoring our pleadings. Tall, thin, rimless glasses and a fedora, Dad always looked like a university English professor. Now, he looked like he failed his son.

Seth lied to everyone about his sexual involvement with Parkman, not just his father. The lies appeared to destroy Seth as much as the sex destroyed him. The more pressure put on Seth to disclose, the more he was forced to lie; to us, his father, the police, and his friends. Seth was living a constant lie and falling apart, but Parkman was more controlling than ever and unconcerned about Seth's deterioration.

CHAPTER 16

I called Lieutenant Somerset regarding the Superintendent's continued visits to Seth.

"Oh, I know," said Somerset wearily. "I'm now hearing from store owners, restaurant managers, and other people around town that the Superintendent has a young boyfriend."

Somerset came to school to meet with me and A.P. Christopher. The three of us met in Christopher's tiny office. We had to ask the office secretary to leave, allowing three of us to fit more comfortably. We again examined the permission forms signed by Seth's Dad, allowing Parkman to legally remove Seth from school. As long as Dad signed, the police were blocked.

Somerset updated us on the police investigation. As a result of my recent meeting with Dad, he finally expressed concern to the police and permitted another interview of Seth.

"How come Mr. Cohen is concerned enough to call the police," Dad asked Somerset. The Lieutenant explained it was my job to protect students and in so doing, Somerset exposed my whistle-blowing to Seth. Two hours later, Seth told Parkman I'd gone to the police. My life was about to change even more.

99

The next afternoon, Parkman charged into my office red-faced and slammed the door. He sat at my conference table and stared at me. Just when I thought he would scream, he shocked me by sobbing, again.

"I thought we were friends and you go and report me to the police," he said through tears.

I tried to present a rationale for my police report, but it was impossible to communicate with him on any normal level. He could not accept that I might have saved his job and family by taking my concerns to the police. We argued and he left my office in tears. Parkman was beginning a long, steep demise. Was Parkman crying because he lost me as a friend? I think not. Initially, I thought he cried because we were trying to separate him from Seth. Much later, I realized his crying was more about the consequences he knew he'd ultimately face because of what he'd already done.

I felt like Hemingway's old man at sea. We had finally sunk the hook into Parkman's jowl and could now start a long haul, reeling him in but with a great struggle. Parkman, like the old man's fish, was fighting what could only be a losing struggle. I knew he thought he'd get away from us, but the hook was in deep. He seemed totally lost. This gave us the impetus to attack stronger.

Dr. Guevara began pressing Seth harder for information, knowing Seth would complain to Parkman about the probing questions. Guevara thought the questions might frighten Parkman away. Although Guevara always couched his concerns within the framework of counseling, Seth always saw through the façade and reported to Parkman that Guevara was continuously "snooping." Parkman feared Guevara because, years earlier regarding another complex case, I had described Guevara as a brilliant psychologist.

Again, Parkman demanded I help him retaliate against Guevara. He directed me to review Guevara's daily records and request logs of all his sessions.

"I will not. The laws require his logs remain totally confidential between therapist and student. Why would you want me to do that? It would be illegal and you and I would both get in trouble."

"What do you mean me," he joked. But, he directed me to request Guevara's logs.

"Why," I asked.

He started screaming.

"Guevara is trying to fabricate a sexual relationship between Seth and me."

"You've got bigger problems than Guevara," I yelled back. "Half the teachers are upset about your relationship with Seth."

"I expect you to fight the teachers for me while I put a stop to Guevara's constant nagging of Seth."

"This battle can only be won by you staying away from our school."

"I'm the Superintendent and I'll do what I damn please."

"You'll 'damn please' yourself right out of a job and a family."

Guevara and I later analyzed this screaming match and he suggested an even stronger psychological confrontation with Parkman. At the same time, I felt my confrontations no longer mattered to Parkman. I needed to expand the "attack" team but none of my three assistant principals could risk involvement. They were not tenured. Parkman could fire any one of them who spoke to him as I did. I needed Guevara's involvement in a confrontation. He was tenured and ready.

CHAPTER 17

The next day, my union attorney, Bush, called. He was a tall, thin man who always looked like a Philadelphia lawyer; every hair in place, navy pin-striped suit and highly polished shoes. I knew his office and car were not cluttered like mine. I'd been impressed with Bush at a recent workshop he'd conducted and had high expectations.

"This is a very sad memo, indeed, that you wrote about Parkman. What do you want to do?" he asked.

"I called you because you're my lawyer. *You* tell *me* what to do."

"Where do you want to go with this?"

"Do I need to tell the State Commissioner?"

"Have you seen anything sexual to report?" he asked.

Bush seemed frightened by the possibility that I was crazy. I was surprised that he didn't believe me. He wanted to call the school district's lawyer, Kevin Miller, to verify my story. That concerned me.

"What if they retaliate against me because I went to you? I'm not sure Miller is the way to go."

"What do you want to do with this information?"

I did not know how to respond. I thought he would guide me. Instead, he kept asking me what I wanted to do.

"You're my lawyer. If you think we should tell Parkman's lawyer what we're doing, then speak with him. But I know he'll tell Parkman."

I could tell from Bush's attitude that he did not believe my written observations of Parkman.

"Should I call the Commissioner's office," I asked again. He responded as I had come to expect.

"If that's what you want to do, you can, but you are not required to do anything because you have no real sense of anything sexual happening."

"I only have concerns, no evidence, and I've reported my concerns to the police."

"There's nothing else you have to do but I'd like to call Kevin Miller, the district's lawyer, with your permission."

"If you think we should call Miller, then do it," I told him.

When Bush phoned, Miller was meeting with Board President Fletcher about my memo.

"I'll call you right back," said Miller, "after Dr. Fletcher finishes telling me about Cohen's memo."

Fifteen minutes later, Miller returned the call to Bush.

"I'm with the Board President right now and he has filled me in on Cohen's memo. Tell Mr. Cohen we are aware of Parkman's relationship with the boy and that Parkman has been directed to cease the relationship or face consequences. Tell Mr. Cohen to be quiet about this because it's under control."

Bush relayed this to me, adding; "You have done all you need do if you reported to your supervisor, to the Board President and the police." He nervously reiterated Miller's claim that Parkman was under control and I should be quiet or perhaps get fired. I wanted no part of being quiet.

Bush warned I might be charged with "interfering in the operation of a school district." But, Guevara and I had to confront Parkman before more wagons circled around him and rallied players against me. I called Parkman's secretary, and asked if his afternoon schedule was full. "Not at all," she responded.

I told Rosa I had a surprise for Parkman. "Please don't tell him I'm on my way over." She agreed. Guevara cancelled his appointments and we went to confront our boss about his relationship with a child. We questioned the sanity of our actions but knew we had to confront him because nobody was intervening.

Parkman's office was a huge room with a ten-person conference table, a settee replete with communications technology and a side-desk holding two separate PC's and a lap-top, all of which seemed buried under a sea of peripheral gadgets. Parkman sat at his desk, almost 15 yards from the door.

"May I come in," I said as I stuck my head into his office. He waved me in and said he had a question about his new camera. I told him, "hold onto the question," and waved Dr. Guevara to follow me into Parkman's office. I then pulled the plunger on the explosive.

"We're here to confront you about your inappropriate behavior with our student, Seth," I boldly announced. The Superintendent cocked his head and looked at me sideways with a questioning glance. I was again challenging him about Seth but this time in the presence of a staff member he distrusted. He said nothing, but held out both his hands to invite more remarks. Guevara took the Superintendent's cue and approached Parkman's desk almost at a run.

"Whose emotional needs are really being met when you come over to the school and leave the building with Seth during school hours?" Parkman raised his eyebrows in surprise at Guevara's psychological boldness. Trying to disarm us, he gestured to the two empty chairs at his desk. We sat but stayed strong.

"Can you respond to that or do you not know?" I added.

"My therapist asked me that very same question," he answered, leaning back in his executive chair. I jumped at the mention of his therapist.

"As long as you're the one who broke confidentiality about your therapy, can you tell us what you told the therapist about Seth?"

Parkman leaned forward with both hands palm-down on the desk as if to ground himself. He was in a white shirt, tie and suit pants. His suit jacket was neatly on a nearby hanger. He loosened his tie and suddenly a tear edged out of one eye.

"I promised my therapist I'd try to separate from Seth as quickly as possible. But, I'm so convinced the boy needs me now more than ever," he sobbed, "that I don't want to abandon him. His mother abandoned him. The school system abandoned him. His father is abandoning his responsibilities. I don't know if I can also abandon him even though I told my therapist I would."

Guevara and I were disarmed by his honesty. My jaw hung open but we had a plan and now was the time.

"I know you trust me," I told Parkman. "So why not let us take over the boy's mentoring? Between me and Dr. Guevara, we can handle it and you can get out of Seth's life without worrying about him. End the obsession. Give yourself a chance to think about other things."

Guevara added, "I don't mean to brag, but Mr. Cohen has shared with me that you have a very high regard for my skills as a psychologist. I will commit myself to Seth's emotional well-being and Mr. Cohen will commit himself to Seth's academic success. We'll do this and you can stop seeing the boy immediately. He won't be abandoned."

This was such a reasonable offer that Parkman looked frightened.

"I'll think about that," he answered, but then asked, "Why are you two so concerned and what do you perceive as inappropriate about my relationship with Seth?"

"We are prepared to answer that question. Dr. Guevara will respond regarding the psychological aspects and I will respond regarding Seth's education."

Guevara then gave Parkman a mini-lecture. He reviewed the parentalizing of Seth, emphasizing that Seth was in charge of himself because Parkman's gifts and attention render Seth's Dad useless in his role as supervisor. Guevara also discussed the adultifying of Seth by having a 54-year-old best-friend.

I then spoke about Parkman's undermining of Seth's educational progress. I explained how his rescues destroy Seth's personal survival mechanisms by enabling him to rely on Parkman. Guevara spoke again about Seth's need for independent growth, while Parkman listened and agreed with every one of Guevara's points.

I then asked Parkman a question to which I knew the answer, "How does your family feel about your relationship with Seth?"

Parkman may have been honest about his obsession but he lied about his family's concerns.

"They love Seth and are considering including him in more of our family activities."

I wanted to protect his daughter and wife and not disclose they had both expressed concerns to me. If I told him I spoke with his family, we would have had another screaming confrontation and lost the opportunity to help Seth. But, our concerns were legitimate and a screaming match with Parkman really wasn't a big deal anymore. We had to go full throttle. I let it happen.

"Your family has complained to me about Seth always being there as if he were a family member. They are very unhappy about Seth."

Parkman looked skeptical, so I went further, giving him enough information to prove his family had discussed Seth with me. I told Parkman that I'd heard about him and Seth raking leaves together, cleaning the car, and having Seth in the house invading their early-morning weekend privacy.

"They feel angry that they must wear bathrobes over their nightgowns or pajamas when they get out of bed on weekends because Seth might be there, even at 7:00 a.m."

"She's too immodest and sexy anyway," Parkman answered, "She *should* wear a robe."

Where were his values? I was trying to communicate about his family's concerns and he was commenting about his daughter's lingerie. He then ranted about contemporary teenage girls' immodesty, avoiding discussion of his family's concerns.

Months earlier, several teachers were with me in the school corridor when Parkman made an unsavory remark about a passing girl's immodest attire. Nobody in earshot responded to his boorish suggestion that she needed breast reduction surgery. The teachers later agreed it was a statement they'd rather not hear from their School Superintendent. It spoke reams but we didn't know it.

Guevara and I left the Superintendent's office but only after more tears from Parkman and his promise to further discuss the relationship with his shrink. He did not agree to have me and Guevara take over his mentoring. In leaving, I took a parting shot.

"Try to figure out if you care more about Seth or your family because you are so obsessed with Seth that you may soon have to choose between him and your family."

Parkman had enough. He stood and pointed at me but before he could say anything, Guevara interrupted.

"Well, that may be going too far," attempting to mollify Parkman's sudden anger. "But, you really do need to be discussing this with your shrink," he added, as we quickly left.

We went outside to the parking lot and stood there staring at the blackbirds gathering in the trees for the evening.

"I think he's fucking this kid," Guevara finally said.

"We're dead, now," I added. "He won't give up the boy and now he won't give up his fight against us. He knows we are his enemy. He's in love and we're dead."

"We're dead," Guevara agreed.

CHAPTER 18

The conflict between Seth's intellect and his emotions started in third grade. With above-average intelligence, he knew right from wrong but behaved very independently even when his intellect told him his behaviors were not what teacher expected. He was always tall and thin, like his father, a build that caused high athletic expectations among friends and teachers. Seth always disappointed them because he had neither the interest in sports nor the home experiences leading to sports.

Seth's dad described a home with a counter-culture lifestyle, emphasizing that Seth and his sisters were different from other neighborhood youngsters in the academic and literary sense. Their household marched to its own drummer. Seth and his sisters felt empowered to be unusual and the boy's friendship with a man was acceptable because it was "unusual."

Seth was aware that he and Bob had become too friendly for their age difference even before the relationship became sexual. He testified that he enjoyed the status and power that went along with being the Superintendent's friend but he knew they were discussing things that were inappropriate.

Even after I confronted him with Guevara, Parkman decided to share with me that Seth was uncomfortable discussing his sexual development. It was these very disclosures by Parkman that kept prompting me to stop the man-boy relationship. After I again suggested he leave such topics to Guevara, Parkman proudly explained how he broke Seth's reluctance to discuss personal matters by emphasizing the concept of inter-generational friendship. When I shared this "inter-generational friendship" rationale with Detective Robinson, he told me the term was a rationale put forth by NAMBLA, the man-boy love association.

As Spring approached, Seth's father repeatedly questioned Seth about his departures from school and his after-school visits to District headquarters. Seth continued to defend Parkman. He truly felt Parkman wanted to help him, even after that their relationship had become sexual. He expected Parkman to change his life in ways beyond sex.

Even with my constant derision, Parkman spoke with me of little else than Seth. He now tried to reinforce the notion of "mentoring" by explaining he was using a play-therapy model to engage Seth in productive discussion.

"Seth, let's see what the latest news is on Yahoo!" Or, he would ask Seth to check his stocks that day. Seth responded positively to any lead-in that engaged him with Bob's high-end technology. The young boy felt important sitting with the School Superintendent at the technological helm of his school district.

The more Parkman's staff saw Seth in Parkman's office, the more negative they felt about the relationship. Parkman was unaware he was the butt of whispered ridicule at District headquarters. Eventually, most of his staff mentioned their concerns to

Parkman because his obsession was blatant and embarrassing to all. Each of Parkman's staff testified at Grand Jury that they warned Parkman about his relationship with Seth. Seth testified differently.

"They may have warned him, but these people saw me at headquarters, two or three times a week when I was still in eighth grade. Nobody on the Superintendent's staff seemed to mind me being there. Nobody seemed to care that I was working in his office after school. But 'work' was really just for us to be together."

District staff could not report illegal behavior because they saw none. If Parkman was inappropriate with Seth at District headquarters it was never visible. One of Parkman's assistants testified he saw them together at a local diner after Parkman received a directive from Fletcher to stay away from Seth.

"I felt sick, like I was seeing something dirty, something I shouldn't be seeing," he moaned. Parkman testified he thought it sad that members of his Cabinet were upset enough to express their concerns to him but never worried enough to report to authorities.

"I guess they trusted me."

On the Superintendent's birthday, Parkman's Cabinet sat around his desk in a semicircle so they could present him with gifts. The first gift came from an assistant, Dick DiNapoli, who also served as the District's Sexual Harassment Monitor.

DiNapoli rose from his chair at the end of the semicircle, offered his gift to Parkman, and held out his arms for a hug. Paul Bernstein, another Cabinet member remarked:

"Bob, you can kiss him. He won't charge you with sexual harassment." Bernstein then turned to the group and quipped:

"He's not going to kiss him. DiNapoli's not Seth." Parkman gave a stern look.

This kind of joking was routine when they had the protection of the group's presence. With humor, they would try to get Parkman to realize how he was being perceived. Alone with Parkman, however, each was more serious about community perception. He ignored them as he ignored everyone.

Parkman's family grew more concerned about his mental health as the school year progressed. He was falling apart emotionally and no longer able to handle the daily stress of a superintendency. I felt he seemed constantly overcome with fear of being exposed by Seth.

Again, Linda brought her concerns to me. She saw the gifts her husband gave Seth and constantly heard from her friends about community perception. At a Parkman backyard cookout, she said, "Bob wanted to invite Seth but was afraid of what you'd say." We talked at length. She was surprised to learn that she knew about Seth long before I did.

"That's all he talked about at home, so we were certain you knew about Seth all that time." She was highly suspicious when I told her I'd not met Seth until May of his eighth grade. She suddenly spoke very nervously. A registered nurse and community organizer, she never before seemed ill at-ease.

"From Seth's seventh grade on, Bob told me you've been with him when he's been out with Seth."

We stared at each other for ten seconds without speaking. We both then knew there was a serious problem because we now knew that Parkman was covering-up very early in the relationship. We agreed not to confront him regarding his cover-up. We also agreed to be more vigilant and to stay in-touch.

Parkman had used me to validate his sick relationship to his family because I was trusted by them. This meant he had early thoughts that required masking.

Lynn also came back to me, complaining that her father continued to include Seth in everything they did, even personal family events. Only 17, Lynn recognized a serious issue.

"I can't even trust my father with personal information anymore. He'll tell Seth and Seth tells everyone at school."

Lynn spoke with a school counselor about her father's obsession. Although her concerns were confidential, anytime there is possible sexual abuse, the counselor must legally break confidentiality to bring such information to the principal. I advised the counselor to ask Lynn if she ever saw any sexual behavior. Her reports were negative. Parkman was careful at home as well as at school.

CHAPTER 19

Only Seth and the Superintendent knew the relationship had become sexual prior to high school. But, very quickly, Seth's High School teachers began to react publicly with their suspicions of abuse. Several came to my office to express their concerns. After meeting with them, and knowing their penchant for open discussion, I needed to let all the High School teachers know I was fighting to protect Seth. I couldn't make any public pronouncements. I made a plan to rally teacher opposition to Parkman without making any statements about him or Seth.

At the next faculty meeting, with no direct reference to the Superintendent, I conducted training to clarify inappropriate teacher-student activities. I reminded the faculty that I'd already reported several staff to the Superintendent because they had students in their homes or cars without permission or because they had met a student outside of school for non-school reasons.

At the same meeting, I commended one teacher, Mrs. Robins, for taking a child to the emergency room in her car after the child fell on a field trip to West Point. I used this as a rare acceptable reason for having a student in your personal vehicle. The rules were clear.

"It is shocking to me that four staff who resigned in recent years were not in unexpected situations with students. They actually *created* the situations." I reviewed the cases, describing the behaviors that got the teachers in trouble.

Within a week of this training, ten teachers had come to my office to complain about the Superintendent removing Seth from school.

"I would get fired for that same behavior," they all said. They quoted my statements and descriptions from the faculty meeting.

My seed had sprouted. The teachers were angry and vocal.

I could not tell the teachers that I'd already reported Parkman to the police or that we were monitoring him. I told very few people about the police because the Superintendent started publicly attacking me. I did not want that to get worse. He made "Bernie bashing" statements at principals' meetings, parent gatherings and awards dinners. He would publicly chastise me for the most inane reason, usually making himself look silly, but only he didn't realize his silliness. He was in his own paranoid world. The entire community now knew of the man-boy rumors, and knew he bashed me because I was trying to break his hold on Seth.

Teachers began purposely standing in the lobby of the school, watching Parkman come and go. He was oblivious. The lobby had long been a social area for students. Suddenly, groups of teachers were always there, keeping tabs on Parkman's arrivals and departures. They openly discussed the relationship.

Several teachers were very outspoken, especially a popular coach who Parkman chastised for public foul language. Their anger grew as Parkman visited more frequently. Corridor gossip was so rampant that students were able to connect the gossip to stories their parents brought to the dinner table. Within a few months, more than a dozen students had also come to me with concern for Seth.

"Mr. Cohen, I need to tell you something I'm hearing because I want to make sure you've heard it." Another student said, "Mr. Cohen, it sounds like the stories my mom is hearing at her supermarket job are true. Somebody has got to help Seth." Students were repulsed by the rumors and concerned for Seth. The pariah had become popular as a victim and a cause célèbre, but never knew how many students cared about him.

I told students there was a full investigation in progress. I could tell them no more. I wanted the students to know I'd already gone to the police but I didn't want them to hear it from me. I then told certain staff about my police reports because teachers were loudly rebelling against the Superintendent's behavior and I wanted them to know I was working to stop him. I did not want staff to be concerned I was covering up for Parkman because we had been friends. I needed the teachers to know I'd taken action, that we were all opposed to Parkman's behavior.

I shared the specifics about my police reports with several gossipy teachers, knowing they would repeat it to all who would listen. In a short time, most of our teachers and more astute students knew I had reported the Superintendent's actions to the police and to Board President Fletcher. Now, even Parkman learned from the District lawyer that I'd gone to Fletcher and the police.

Fletcher felt he knew Parkman better than I and saw him as "a devout Christian who'd never harm a fly." Fletcher was the intellectual darling of a local business network that controlled Democrat *and* Republican politics in Clearwater. He was a strong public advocate for education. The District had significantly improved under his leadership.

Favorable school reports allowed local realtors to raise home prices and bring higher income residents into the District with their higher achieving children and larger pockets. Clearwater's Mayor, Joe Stevens, publically credited the improved High School and his parks for the housing boom in what had been a long-distressed city. Dozens of students transferred back into Clearwater High School from nearby parochial schools. Fletcher and many others feared that rumors of Parkman's misconduct would hurt this progress.

Successful schools meant higher income residents and more successful businesses. Local commerce rallied to do damage control regarding the Parkman rumors. Business and political leaders met privately with school board members. They tried to prevent the District's reputation from sinking. When they learned I blew the whistle on Fletcher and my supervisors for ignoring my concerns, they joined Parkman's attacks on me. They were not concerned about education or about Seth. They were only worried about Clearwater's growing economy.

They slashed away at my reputation, hoping to undermine the credibility of my reports. They were desperate to protect the District's improved status and their growing businesses.

I knew Parkman would eventually get caught were he guilty. Authorities would then want to learn who knew what, when. I knew I was the only school administrator who went to Fletcher, to the police, and to others with concerns about Parkman. Yet, I also knew I'd be fighting against the same people I had tried to catalyze into action, because they would deny I brought my concerns to them.

CHAPTER 20

After months of monitoring Parkman's arrivals and departures at the High School, Guevara pushed me to confront him again. No authority was stopping him. He had free reign with Seth and Seth was being destroyed. It was time for us to do something more dramatic because the police, the School Board and Seth's dad were unable to stop Parkman.

I spoke with Seth's dad again, just prior to my next confrontation with Parkman. I told him about the frequency of Parkman's visits and their lengthy disappearances. He was shocked. Immediately after finishing with Dad, I went to Parkman's office without an appointment. I was very direct with him after charging past his secretary and slamming the door.

"The entire school is ready to mobilize against you because you continue to take Seth from school without parental consent. I just spoke with Seth's dad. He removed you from Seth's list of authorized adults. You can no longer legally remove him from school." Parkman stood his ground. He jumped from his chair, red-faced and spitting.

"I don't care what you or anybody else thinks. I am mentoring this child and nothing more. What if I had decided to mentor some highly academic, successful student? Nobody would care. This is what happens when I reach into the gutter for some poor slob who has no money and who is the butt of everything bad that happens in your school. If I was mentoring the senior class president or the basketball star, nobody would care."

I had seen this show too many times. Again, he tried to rationalize the relationship. For the last time, I reached out to him with several reasons why everyone thought he was obsessed. He argued. I was beyond arguing.

I finally yelled at him and gave him what he deserved about his family and his job. He cried real tears and again blamed the public education system. He gave me a list of baseless reasons why he could not abandon Seth. He and his reasons were pathetic. I knew I had to forcefully tear him from Seth before the worst happened. Only Parkman and Seth knew the sex had already started. We assumed there was sex because of Seth's and Parkman's irrationality. Knowing that murder sometimes follows sexual molestation, we were concerned for Seth's life.

"I am forced by your behavior to campaign for the boy's safety. Teachers would be fired if they did what you are doing."

It was as if I had said nothing. He ignored my accusations and directed me to make a list of teachers in our school who were talking about him. I was trying to converse with someone who seemed to have a thought-disorder. He was so emotionally paralyzed by his prior deeds that my words weren't heard. The more I accused him of destroying Seth's education and jeopardizing his own family, the less he seemed to hear. He refused to address any issue I raised. He only counter-attacked and threatened me. It was clear that we would fight for our professional lives on this issue.

"My last word of advice to you is to write an explanation of your behavior to Board President Fletcher because teachers from our school will be in his office tomorrow to complain about your behavior." As I left, I turned to him.

"Don't defend your behaviors on the basis of Seth's needs. Examine your own behavior rather than his. You know you're wrong."

I left Parkman's office and went to his assistant's office, offering one last chance for him to help us protect Seth. Like everyone at headquarters, Ross decried Parkman's behavior but saw no way to legally intervene. Everyone knew what had to be done but Seth was the only one who could end it.

After I left Ross, he immediately went to Parkman and informed him of all I had said. From prison, Parkman later testified that none of his Cabinet members kept my meetings confidential. Each time I reached out to one of his Cabinet for help, they went to him with my concerns.

I returned to the High School and met with Intern Garton, who listened incredulously as I reviewed my meetings with Parkman and Ross.

"Seth's teachers are ready to rebel," she interjected. "Those teachers never lose sight of Seth's needs."

I knew Garton was right. Several of the teachers who were ready to speak publicly against the Superintendent had come to my office describing the horrible effect Parkman was having on Seth. They were convinced that Seth was emotionally suffering and they blamed Parkman's involvement, sex or no sex.

Dr. Guevara was prepared to risk his job by addressing the school board about Parkman's behavior and its effect on Seth. Guevara felt he and I had to go public to support Seth's high school teachers. Even if the sex had not happened, we felt Parkman's departures with Seth were inappropriate enough to warrant a public report to the Board.

I called Guevara to join a Cabinet meeting. When he arrived, I telephoned Board President Fletcher on speakerphone.

"What's been done in the past month since we met to discuss Parkman? Parkman continues to remove Seth from the building and weeks have passed since I told teachers that I'd brought our concerns to you."

I went on to explain our next move. "Ten teachers are planning to attend the next school board meeting and three will speak to complain about Parkman's behavior and the Board's lack of response to our call for help. That's how frightened we are by Parkman's obsessive behavior regarding Seth."

"Who is leading this revolution?" Fletcher boldly asked.

Guevara raised his hand.

I informed Fletcher the so-called "revolution" had taken on a life of its own because of Parkman's brashness.

"The Superintendent's tact is to be very public about his relationship with Seth and, therefore, make us think he has nothing to hide. But the boy seems increasingly emotionally dysfunctional because of Parkman's attention."

Fletcher asked me if I could control the group that was rebelling. Everyone at the table shook their heads and smiled, hearing a sudden trepidation in Fletcher's voice.

"I agree with them," I responded. "Why should I try to control them?"

He became unnerved.

"Who can I speak with at the school to inform the group about the steps I'm taking to stop Parkman?"

"You should drop everything and speak with Dr. Guevara unless you want ten or more high school staff pointing fingers at the next school board meeting. They know I reported his behavior to you."

Thirty minutes later, Fletcher arrived at the school. He hadn't even taken time to get out of his optician garb. He told me about his plans for an upcoming meeting with district lawyers. I was disheartened because it was obvious that Fletcher hoped the Parkman issue would disappear and only now, a month later, was having a meeting.

"It's been nearly a month since we spoke about worse case scenarios and you are now first meeting with attorneys?" I asked. "It's no wonder the teachers think we should take matters into our own hands . . . You do not think this could really be happening, do you?"

"I guess I wish it weren't happening. It just seems so impossible if you know him."

I brought Fletcher to Guevara's tiny office, large enough for a desk, file cabinet and two chairs that almost pressed up against the desk. I had prepared Guevara for Fletcher's visit, urging him to be honest and serious in expressing his concerns.

"Take as much time as you guys want and call me if you need my input to this discussion."

I backed out of Guevara's office, noticing that both doctors, the optician and the psychologist, were surprised to be left alone with each other.

"I think you guys can handle this without me,"

After the meeting, Fletcher came to my office, quite shaken. I excused myself from a meeting and met with him in the corridor. I explained to Fletcher that it was necessary for him to hear our concerns from another staff member, without input from me, so he would understand I was not alone in this.

Fletcher was very nervous.

"Guevara is convinced that Parkman already is or will soon be having sex with the boy."

As we spoke, Fletcher fidgeted and showed physical mannerisms I had never seen in the usually sophisticated, confident leader. Fletcher knew he had to make a choice that would see his leadership grow or fail.

"I will take immediate action as I promised Dr. Guevara. I will be in touch with you tomorrow." He left the building at a quick pace. Guevara and I immediately shared notes regarding our separate meetings with Fletcher.

"I thought you were going to be in the meeting with us," Guevara said, quizzically.

"I wanted Fletcher to feel pincers coming from more than one side because I haven't been able to goad him into action."

An hour later, Fletcher telephoned to reassure me he'd take immediate action. I sensed he'd spoken with lawyers and was now being guided by them. His words were very staged. He asked me to "control the revolution" and give him at least one day to explore options with the district's lawyer. I shared that information with my Cabinet and Dr. Guevara. Garton shared it with the rebelling teachers. The following day, Fletcher phoned.

"I spent the entire day with Kevin Miller to come up with a plan that would let Parkman know, once and for all, he needed to leave this boy alone."

The result of Fletcher's meeting with Miller was a letter to Parkman directing him to cease and desist his relationship with Seth or lose his job. This was the "control" they had described months earlier to lawyer Bush, but hadn't yet implemented.

I had no reason to think any action would keep Parkman from Seth. The depth of this problem needed more than a letter because we observed Seth's behavior on a daily basis. Parkman's outrageous fears of gossip made him look paranoid enough to add further credibility to our concerns.

After Parkman's arrest, the entire community saw Fletcher's letter to Parkman because it was published on the front page of the local newspaper. The letter accused Parkman of "educational interference." It said nothing about him removing a child from school or about any other improper behavior. It did right by directing Parkman not to see the boy at the risk of losing his job, but it only stated he was interfering "with our educational plan for Seth." It did not allude to the rumors about the relationship. They were "afraid of hurting Parkman's chances for another job," as they stated to reporters about the weakness of the letter.

Miller and Fletcher told Parkman the letter resulted from my reports to them. The day after he received the letter, Parkman came racing into my office. He sat quickly and slammed his hand on the table. He pointed at me and yelled.

"You know about the Fletcher letter."

I denied knowledge of any letter. He leaned forward and glared at me.

"I-know-you-know-about-the-Fletcher-letter."

"Stop playing head games and just tell me why you came here," I yelled back.

"I am no longer permitted to see Seth. It was presented to me in writing. I was told this is your doing." I stared back at him and eventually spoke. I took a stand.

"Bob, you need to be thanking me for saving your job and career because if you have not already had sex with this boy, you're bound to be inside his pants soon. It's just written all over you. You should not be taking the boy out of school. You should not be having the boy in your car. I would have been fired by you long ago if I did any of those things. You should be thanking me for saving your career and family rather than yelling at me for stopping you."

Parkman felt the letter violated his personal and professional rights.

"I should be allowed to mentor this boy. I have done nothing wrong. You took some kid out to Adelphi University last summer to their summer basketball practice to get him a scholarship. There's no difference between me taking Seth in my car a few times and you taking that kid 50 miles away to a college?"

I pointed out that Mark, our former star basketball player, had graduated two years earlier and was a 21-year-old transferring junior college student, not a 14-year old with issues.

"I took Mark for a tryout and possible scholarship to a college where I know the coach, not to dinner or to buy him underwear like you did with Seth."

"I see no fucking difference," Parkman exploded.

If he saw no difference, I knew he was either very lost in fantasy or lying. Turns out he was both.

I was not going to be a slave to his insanity. Parkman was getting sicker by the day.

"That's why you're a sick puppy, Bob," I teased, trying to make the discussion lighter. He was still my boss and he did not feel humored. He responded with threats.

"Wait until people around town hear that you took this kid in your car out to Adelphi," he said, trying to scare me.

"The kid is no kid, so drop it," I yelled back. "Bob, I have nothing to hide, no reason to be on the defense. So, if you publicly war with me, it's going to be me attacking you about Seth. Attack me for taking a 21-year old to meet my former college coach and you'll look like an ass."

"I'll find some things to attack. That will not be difficult." A prophetic warning to which I paid no heed.

Parkman left the High School having declared war against me. I knew he would not stop seeing Seth. If he was giving me up, one of his few good friends, to stay involved with a 14-year-old boy, I knew he was lost. I concluded that Guevara was right. They were probably already having sex. Parkman could not release the boy for fear he'd tell all.

My former friend now hated me. Fletcher wasn't too happy with me, either, after Guevara and I forced him to act on our suspicions rather than wait for real proof. I could empathize with Fletcher and those who had difficulty accepting our fears. We knew it seemed preposterous to any who did not see Seth and Parkman's respective demises.

I lost hope that my union lawyer would help. He never believed my reports and handed me over on a platter to the District lawyer and Parkman's wrath. Who could believe such accusations? Nobody! I understood why most people thought we were either crazy or political in reporting our Superintendent who appeared to others as totally righteous.

The union lawyer's advice: "Cooperate with the District or they will fire you and I won't be able to help you." We needed more help.

Guevara and I knew the situation required the involvement of another authority. The struggle to expose Parkman was getting so nerve-wracking, that Guevara led us in periodic relaxation, lots of prayer and meditation. My team communicated with each other constantly. Garton, Norris, Guevara, Nelson, and others; we looked in on each other all day. It was maddening. We took risks by going to others. Now we had to protect ourselves as well as Seth.

Guevara recorded a poem/song for me to use as a mantra, "The Fog of War." He also brought me a copy of *High Noon* to watch as motivation to keep fighting.

The local police were the only authorities that believed us but they were stopped by lack of disclosure from Seth. Again I called Child Protective Services for assistance. Again, they said they'd only investigate a report of sex abuse by family members and could not help. When I told them I'd already followed their earlier advice to call local police, they suggested calling the State Police which I did and was told it was a matter for the local police. So, I called our union again for advice. They told me to "shut up about it before I get fired."

I awoke nightly with the shakes during those weeks. I'd sit in bed immobilized, wondering why nobody in authority would help us save Seth. I began to feel victimized for the first time in my life. All the authorities ignored us.

I chanted often, throughout the day, "Nam myo ho, rengee kyo," a Buddhist chant, and, "God got me to it. God will get me through it." I said those chants thousands of times a day while trying to figure out a way for us to catch Parkman and simultaneously run a school with 2,000 students and 250 staff. My assistant principals and several others picked up much of my work so I could handle the anticipated onslaught from Parkman and could focus on rescuing Seth.

CHAPTER 21

Seth had become a discipline problem and we knew it was Parkman's fault. Every bad-boy in a high school has periodic incidents. Seth was unable to maintain self-control. His disruptions seemed driven by his need for Parkman's rescue.

In Seth's 14-year-old mind, his power was repeatedly demonstrated to the entire school when Parkman came to rescue him. One department chairperson liked to say, "Seth is Parkman's boy-toy, but who's controlling who?"

Dr. Guevara believed that Seth's misconduct and was caused by horrific circumstances created by Parkman. Nobody knew if Parkman was raping Seth, but everybody knew that Seth's outbursts signaled an overwhelming personal issue. Guevara was convinced that Seth's behavior problems could only have been caused by ongoing sexual abuse, but Seth continued to protect Parkman when questioned.

Two weeks after receiving the "cease and desist" letter, Parkman felt he should officially break-up with Seth rather than let Fletcher's letter speak for him. He came to my office full of ambivalence, expressing anger at me but showing a devastating sadness.

His prior visit had been so hostile and threatening that I was surprised by his candor.

"How can I desert this boy? I have not seen Seth since the letter was shoved in my hand by Fletcher and Bradley. I don't take Seth's calls. I don't answer his emails. When he comes to my office after school, the receptionist tells him I'm in meetings and he shouldn't come in the building."

Parkman said he had gained ten pounds in the two weeks since he had last seen Seth. "I guess I'm filling the void," he mused.

Parkman sat at my desk, crying and giving me his sob story while hours earlier he was telling his staff to destroy me.

I offered no solutions when he asked for advice on "abandoning" Seth. He seemed ill, barely able to speak.

"He has no father to speak of. His mother left him. I am all he has and now he lost me."

Parkman left my office in tears. He called me almost daily for a week with sad rantings and spoke about his personal torment. I might have believed him, but friends in his office informed me Parkman regularly told his staff I was after his job and he wanted me fired. I had little tolerance for his rant and cut it short.

We continued to monitor Seth's activities and attendance. If Seth was late to school, we worried that Parkman might have picked him up as he walked. Seth's dad agreed to drive him to school and finally understood that Parkman had already caused emotional harm to Seth, whether or not there had been sex.

Within a few weeks after the split-up, Seth seemed calmer. His improved behavior was a signal that, perhaps, Parkman had stopped imposing himself sexually or was not even seeing Seth. Still, we remained vigilant.

Seth settled into a normal student routine with only rare disruptions. He was now more focused on his schoolwork. Unfortunately, just as Seth was improving, Fletcher gave Parkman permission for a chaperoned "good-bye." Parkman telephoned to inform me that he wanted his meeting with Seth to be at the High School.

After confirming this with Fletcher, I arranged a room for a final farewell. I told Parkman he could not be alone with Seth. Parkman asked me to be the chaperone. I refused.

"Tell me someone else at this school with whom you and Seth would be comfortable and I'll make the arrangements," I told him. He was a pitiful figure, distraught, frightened and verbally inept.

Parkman asked for Marie Pierre, a school counselor who had spent many hours with his daughter, but Pierre also refused. She did not want to participate because of her confidential relationship with Lynn.

I called Parkman to tell him of Pierre's response. He screamed into the phone.

"Damn it, what have you done to me in that building that people will not even spend ten minutes with me."

"Bob, anything that comes to you from people in this building, you brought upon yourself with your own suspicious behavior."

I asked him to suggest another chaperone. He requested Ms. Mendoza, another school counselor. Seth later testified that Mendoza was one of his telephone links to Parkman when he wanted to "report" a teacher or needed to be rescued. Parkman controlled Mendoza. She was angry at me because I replaced her unlicensed brother with a licensed teacher when I came on board. But, I knew she'd not let anything go wrong in that room.

Mendoza agreed to chaperone the "breakup" meeting between Parkman and Seth. I gave her strict guidelines.

"Do not leave them alone for a second, listen carefully to every word that is said, do not engage in any conversation, and tell Parkman when there are two minutes of his ten minutes remaining."

I telephoned Parkman about the bizarre arrangements. Now I was dictating rules to my boss for a break-up meeting with his 14-year-old boyfriend. Parkman was unstable, and my primary focus had to be Seth's safety.

When the Superintendent arrived, I met him in the lobby and spoke with him in the safety of the corridor. I did not want to be alone with him in my office. From the look on his face, I feared a horrible scene were we behind closed doors. It took place anyway. Standing in the corridor, he went into a screaming tirade so loud that nearby offices and classrooms slammed their doors because of his vulgarity.

"It's all because of you that everybody in this fucking town thinks Seth is giving me blow jobs every time I take him in my car. It's your fucking fault that people think I'm fucking him at my house. We have no sex. We have no blow jobs. This is all in your sick imagination."

He continued, even after seeing doors slam shut around us. I took him into my office to allow nearby classes to function. He looked like he might have a total breakdown. He was sweating and his eyes seemed twice normal size. He was a wreck. I knew he could no longer govern a school district. He couldn't even govern his own life. He appeared ready to vomit, clutching his stomach.

Mendoza called to say she had Seth in her office. Parkman started to cry. I gave him a minute to clean up. I called a security guard to escort him. I did not want to be with him another minute.

In Mendoza's office, with security posted outside the door, the three sat around a table after the Superintendent greeted Seth with a handshake.

"You haven't heard from me for several weeks," Parkman started, "because there are people here who feel I am bad for your educational development. They think I've done wrong by removing you from a hostile environment and by, in their opinion, taking control over your behavior that should be in the hands of your teachers and administrators."

Parkman told him their separation need not be permanent. "Those who are responsible for you may feel differently after some time. At this time, I just need to say good-bye until we meet again."

"Why did you come here," Seth asked.

Parkman explained he did not want Seth to feel rejected by him and that he still cared about him but had to follow the directives of the School Board. Seth calmly expressed understanding. According to Mendoza, Seth seemed more stable than Parkman. Seth did what he could to make the Superintendent feel less guilty about the separation.

"I'll be okay, Bob. I really will be okay. Don't worry about me. If we ever get together again, I hope people understand."

Mendoza also reported that Seth seemed relieved by the break-up. Dr. Guevara interpreted Seth's relief as a signal of earlier sexual abuse by Parkman. If so, we hoped that Seth's relief would eventually allow him to disclose.

CHAPTER 22

Parkman became more public with his barbs against me. Our relationship became an all-out public war with Seth as the prize. Although Parkman had officially been stripped of his ability to see Seth, he did not give up his quest to renew that relationship and to destroy me for interfering.

Seth was a much more capable student and socially-competent teen without Parkman in his life. Parkman, however, became totally incompetent without Seth.

Seth was now able to focus on his teachers and his friends with fewer incidents. Parkman worried so much about Seth disclosing their sexual activities that he could focus on little else.

We could now prevent Parkman from seeing Seth in our school, but we had no authority outside the building. If the School Board and police could not keep them apart, how could we?

Then it hit me. I quickly called a Cabinet meeting.

""Because he is our boss, we do not have the power to make Parkman disappear but we can make Seth disappear. Seth's recent behavior qualifies him for Bedford High School, the county's alternative high school for students with self-management issues.

He'll get daily counseling and he'll be ten miles away from Clearwater." The Cabinet agreed.

We knew Parkman would fight the transfer but I felt Seth's dad could be pressured to agree. If we convinced Dad of the transfer, we could get Seth far away from Parkman for most of the day. Seth would be on an early bus to a distant school with a long day. Parkman could not get to him in transit, and would not start visiting Bedford.

Dr. Guevara met with Seth's teachers, all of whom would need to support the transfer. His teachers agreed that Bedford would give Seth an opportunity to grow on his own, away from Parkman. Unfortunately, Parkman and his cabinet were our main hurdles to the transfer because several of them had voting power on the transfer. All transfers to Bedford required the Superintendent's approval because the transfer had budget ramifications. The Clearwater District paid Bedford per student.

That week, just before the transfer meeting, we felt Parkman was seeing Seth because both had reprised their most outrageous acts. Seth became disruptive in the café after a calm two months and Parkman was almost non-functional, barely able to carry on a conversation. Although months had passed since he had been given the "cease and desist" letter, daily sightings of the couple were reported. The transfer had to happen.

Parkman had become a pariah. Even his own staff stayed away from him. Appointments to see the Superintendent were no longer necessary. You could meet with him any time you showed up at his office because he had nothing to do. He had emotionally collapsed. He sat there, alone, all day. Fortunately for the children of Clearwater, his cabinet did his work and kept the Clearwater

School District functioning. Principals stopped visiting for consultations. Parents of students, so repulsed by the rumors, no longer called him about their own child's problems. He was totally isolated and in constant fear of Seth's disclosure.

Some felt Parkman's collapse meant he was seeing Seth again. Others thought the opposite; that his demise was due to a longing for Seth.

Guevara and I had a third theory. We believed Parkman's total emotional collapse was actually a constant state of panic. No longer able to control Seth, he had an ongoing fear of Seth's disclosure. He seemed like a man awaiting death. Now, by transferring Seth to Bedford, we were about to drag Seth even further away from Parkman's control. I had to meet with Parkman about the transfer. I knew it would not be an easy discussion.

I entered Parkman's office and closed the door, hoping he'd be frightened enough to support Seth's transfer. He looked up from his desk, shrugged his shoulders, and leaned back in his executive chair in a manner which said, "Bring it on." I got straight to the point.

"Since you received the letter barring you from seeing Seth, you've continuously told me how worried you are about his future. As his principal, I am the person who's ultimately responsible for his academic success. Along with his teachers and counselors, we are recommending he transfer to Bedford High School where he'll get continuous support and specialized help in dealing with stress and self-management."

"I won't allow it," he abruptly yelled, sitting upright. I stood my ground.

"This isn't up to you, nor does it concern you. I came here to make sure you don't have an outrageous reaction in front of him which would further delay his progress. The last thing we need is for Seth to feel guilty about leaving you behind," I explained.

"I won't allow it. Don't you hear me? I won't allow it. If it has nothing to do with me, why are you telling me about it?"

I reminded him that a meeting was required to approve the transfer.

"We expect you to have a hostile reaction to the transfer. We want you to have your reaction now, in your office, behind closed doors, so it will not impact Seth or the Committee or his family. Seth needs this transfer to get his life back on track. Stay away from the Committee meeting."

"We'll see," he said menacingly. "I have a right to be there."

I returned to my office and telephoned Seth's dad.

He came to my office two hours later. I taped the meeting with Dad. Although Dad approved the presence of the tape recorder, he asked me to turn it off three times during our conversation when he spoke negatively about Parkman. He was afraid of repercussions against Seth. I explained the transfer rationale.

"We are still worried about the relationship between Parkman and your son. We want to transfer Seth to a different school setting that will improve Seth's future and keep him away from Parkman."

Dad struggled with the concept. I knew I had to be relentless. I made it more personal, hoping to convince him.

"I am concerned that Parkman has taken away your role as his father." Dad's response shocked me.

"What does Mr. Parkman have against you . . . Why is he out to get you?"

"Why do you think Mr. Parkman is out to get me?"

"Can we turn off the tape recorder?"

"Of course."

He described a sickening scenario.

"I was sitting in my car outside the Middle School a couple weeks ago, waiting to pick up my daughter. Parkman saw me and came over to my car. He suggested I contact the New York State Commissioner of Education to report you for mismanaging my son's entire first year of high school. He said he would publicly agree with my report to the Commissioner."

Parkman was moving more aggressively toward my destruction than I'd thought.

"Don't you realize he wants you to report me because I am trying to keep him away from your son?"

Dad was confused.

"Mr. Parkman once told me that you and he were good friends. Seth was still in eighth grade when he told me I shouldn't worry about Seth in high school because Mr. Cohen was the best principal in New York State. He'll make sure Seth is ok."

Because Parkman was now taking steps to destroy me, I was convinced he was still a danger to Seth. Such extremes from Parkman meant he feared a Bedford transfer would result in Seth's disclosure.

It was frightening to realize Parkman was so obsessed with my downfall. I now feared his irrationality toward me as much as I feared his obsession with Seth. The crying, the outrageous anger; he was sinking. This signaled bad days ahead for Seth and for me.

After 90 minutes of my badgering and my repeated threats to report him to CPS for "authorizing" his son's relationship with Parkman, Dad agreed to sign the transfer to Bedford.

CHAPTER 23

The stakes were raised in this battle. It was no longer just about Seth. Now I was also fighting Parkman for my own professional survival and needed a larger army. I could not stop Parkman's constant attacks even with the help from Guevara and my staff.

I called in the President and Vice President of the High School Parents Club. They were well-rooted professionals in Clearwater and might be able to help expand our army. When I asked if they'd heard rumors related to our Superintendent, they responded, "People all over town are gossiping about Parkman and his young boyfriend."

I brought them up to-date on all we had done to intervene with Parkman. I wanted them to tell others about my reports to the Board and to the police. We needed to use their local contacts to find someone who could ensure Seth's safety until the transfer took place. These two community leaders sought other support for me and for Seth via their own full-time leadership positions: a hospital administrator, and a community organizer. It took only a day for their outreach to reach Parkman's ear. When he heard I'd brought parents into the battle, he told his staff I'd gone crazy.

"Cohen is now responsible for the community rumors about me. Now I know he wants my job and will get rid of my staff. You must destroy him now."

That school year ended with a dysfunctional Superintendent, his mind in total disarray, in constant fear of exposure. Key district staff held the school system in place. His Assistant Superintendents carried the weight, filling in for him at most of the end-term public assemblies. However, certain ceremonies required his presence. When that happened and he was forced to make an appearance, he was unable to overcome the inner psychological drain of being Jekyll-Hyde. Very little substance flowed forth.

Parkman lost all sense of public composure, embarrassing himself at his daughter's graduation. His speech to the graduates, inappropriately silly, was interrupted by three phony incoming cell phone calls purportedly from his daughter who was sitting 30 feet away with the grads. Four thousand people in the stadium felt humiliated by his antics at the podium. Only the youngest children appreciated his silly humor. A young child probably helped him write the silliness.

Before summer recess, with a "shock and awe"-type surge, Parkman pushed his staff to send me daily memos and phone calls about sudden budget issues, new staffing problems, scheduling roadblocks, safety reports and every possible demand they could structure at year's end. He told his staff I was ignoring regulations and stealing everything I could. They hounded me and my secretaries for weeks. They grabbed my secretary's petty cash books as if she were a criminal, but found nothing. My staff helped me respond to all their demands.

As of July 1st, Seth was no longer our student. Parkman could not prevent his transfer to Bedford. We had outfought his Cabinet on all transfer-related matters such as Dad's signature and budget for transportation. Guevara organized the committee votes needed from Seth's teachers.

We were certain that Parkman felt Seth's transfer would lead to Seth's disclosure of sex. Because of Parkman's fears, this horrendous school year quickly became a summer battlefield. The rumor-mill had Parkman seeing Seth despite the written prohibition. Ironically, Parkman's contract as Superintendent came due that summer. The School Board gave him a raise and renewed their contract with a Superintendent who had already been told in writing to keep away from a student. The public was not yet aware that Parkman had received the "cease and desist" letter. It is possible that no Board members, other than the two signers, knew of the letter.

I called my Cabinet together for brainstorming. It was like a war room. I made three lists on my easel. Standing next to the easel, I explained:

"Here's a list of what we've done to stop Parkman from having relations with Seth. Here's a list of what we've done to let the authorities know our concern. Here's how we've covered our asses by letting other people know about our reporting."

I continued. "Let's imagine that each person to whom we reported Parkman's behavior lied to us when they said they'd take it to the next step. Let's see where else we must report if our contacts are just sitting on the information because they think we're crazy."

Knowing Parkman as I did, I understood how others could not accept our concerns. Parkman bought gifts for all of us at his annual retreat. He was kind to people around him and always considerate of others. Yet, on a beautiful summer day, we were now meeting to figure out how to protect a kid from him. For the third time, in hope of finding another form of assistance, we reviewed the District Guidelines for Reporting Staff Suspected of Student Sex Abuse.

I called CPS again, this time on speakerphone during the Cabinet meeting. Again, CPS referred us to the police because the abuse was outside the family. If no other agency would help, we had to bring other cops into the situation. I called Somerset's partner, Detective Robinson, and asked to speak with him privately. I thought, as a detective, maybe he had different contacts than Somerset. He came to the school that day. I filled him in on all we had done to document Parkman.

Robinson was stoic. He never commented on what Somerset had or had not shared, but I knew he was hearing some things for the first time. I sensed that his fidgeting was tension about his partner's not having shared all he was now hearing. With Robinson updated, he seemed ready to expand the investigation rather than just hope for Seth's disclosure.

This expanded our avenue with the police. I asked Dr. Guevara to do the next expansion of our reporting because there needed to be official reports from someone other than myself. I wanted higher authorities to know I was not the only person with concerns about Parkman's relationship with Seth. They could think I was crazy or political, but if others were saying the same about Parkman, maybe they'd listen.

Guevara was primed for action. We decided our union attorney was wrong. Contact with the State Education Department was important. Guevara reached out to the State by calling their local representative. In New York, hundreds of school districts are organized as autonomous units with school boards, but they exist in a corporate-style hierarchy wherein *the State* has supervisory oversight via a county structure known as BOCES (Board of Cooperative Education Services). If we needed to report to the State regarding any compliance issue or if the State had concerns about our school, communications always went through the County BOCES Superintendent's office.

Guevara spoke with an Assistant County Superintendent, Dr. Alice Hammer, the individual responsible for investigating State law compliance issues. She taught courses on compliance regulations at a nearby university and was considered a bulldog on such matters as child sex abuse. She and Guevara had two 45-minute, very revealing telephone interviews during which Guevara detailed our observations and concerns. She briefed Dr. Gye, the County Superintendent, who then conducted a lengthy interview with Parkman. After that interview, Parkman came charging into my office.

"I just received a telephone call from Dr. Gye, who questioned me for 30 minutes about my relationship with Seth. I know from his questions that it was either you or Guevara who called and I'm going to conclude it was Guevara from Gye's psychological vocabulary."

"I don't know what you're talking about. Furthermore, why are you even telling me this?"

"I'm telling you this because you need to know I've proven my innocence to the State. I am directing you to tell Guevara that he's not to discuss anything about me unless he wants to get fired."

I gave him a blank stare.

"Did you hear me?"

"You tell Guevara yourself. If you want me to tell Guevara that he's not to discuss you or Seth anymore, put that in writing."

He stood at the end of my conference table and glared again, as he had done so often.

"I am innocent of any misconduct with Seth and you are responsible for the fact that so many people in Clearwater think I am fucking this kid." He pointed at me and walked out saying, "You better watch your back."

Although Guevara had convinced Dr. Hammer of the need for an investigation, Parkman fooled the State Education Department by sweet-talking Dr. Gye.

"Okay," I said to Parkman, "the issue is dead."

"I want to know exactly who reported me to Dr. Gye and I want a list of people who have been talking about me."

He repeated the same request he made months earlier. He seemed harmless, but I was frightened of his team's ability to ruin me. I tried to calm him.

"Let's just say it was me *and* Guevara who made the report and that you convinced the State you're not a pedophile. You should let everyone know that the State has investigated you and everything's fine. I'll even call the newspaper reporter for you."

"Don't be ridiculous. I'm not going to attract attention to this issue by letting people know about the State's investigation."

"Okay, let's summarize," I said. "According to you, you are mentoring Seth and people are misunderstanding your relationship. Rumors started which resulted in reports expressed to me and Guevara. We did our duty by making reports to our supervisors, along with reports to the Board President and the State.

They've interviewed you. You received a letter to stay away from the boy. End of story." I tried to make him think I was putting all this behind me. I knew it wasn't convincing, but I could do nothing else at that point.

CHAPTER 24

Summer contact between Parkman and me was limited. Summer contact between Parkman and anybody was limited. I worked my required ten days and stayed away from him, as did everyone else.

Parkman was depressed and distracted to the point he could no longer do his work. While most people thought his sadness was about losing Seth, Guevara and I still felt his funk was a constant fear of Seth's disclosure. Parkman may have convinced Dr. Gye, but Seth still knew the truth.

Parkman suddenly disappeared for ten days. Nobody knew where he was. Few cared. When he returned, he telephoned and said, "I heard you were looking for me. I needed to get away for a week to clear my head and rebuild my relationship with my family."

He inexplicably disappeared twice more that summer, never even letting his secretary know when he'd be absent.

I was at home during early August when I answered the phone to hear Parkman's very concerned voice.

"Hello, do you have a minute . . . I need your help urgently." I knew this had to be related to Seth.

"What's going on?" I asked.

"I know I convinced *you* that I'm no longer involved with Seth, but I'm deeply concerned about Dr. Guevara. I think he has it out for me. According to the feedback I received from Seth and the State, I need to be very concerned about Guevara."

"What is your concern, Bob?"

"I don't care how confidential you say Guevara's work is, he still makes written records of each session he has with Seth and I'm concerned about some of the things he may have put in writing. Seth told me that Guevara and you were continuously badgering him about his relationship with me. I'm not happy that you did that but he says you didn't take notes. I'm concerned that Guevara may have written some of his crazy ideas about me into Seth's records."

"What do you want me to do?"

"Do you have a key to Guevara's office?"

"I have a key to every lock in the school," I reassured him.

"Do you have a key to his file cabinet?"

"Presumably, I am supposed to be able to open any lock, door or cabinet in my school if there is some kind of emergency." Parkman followed with nothing short of blackmail.

"Well, I know I'm not supposed to have contact with Seth, but I recently bumped into Seth's father who told me he is contacting lawyers and the State Education Commissioner to sue you for mismanaging his son's education. This will destroy your career. You know he's right. You did mismanage Seth's education. But, if Seth's file should suddenly disappear from Guevara's office, I know that Seth's father will not go forward with the lawsuit."

I was stunned. I think my chin hit my knee.

"Bob, are you asking me to steal Seth's record from Guevara's office? What's the point of that? Why would you want that?"

I reminded him that he had just spent time convincing me there was nothing wrong about his relationship with Seth.

"So, why should you be concerned about Guevara's record-keeping?"

Parkman said he was concerned that such records might hurt Seth's future.

"This is not about me," he said. "This is about Seth."

"So you want me to steal Seth's record from Guevara's office?"

He rationalized that it wouldn't be stealing because, as principal I had an obligation to protect Seth, even if the protection meant correcting inaccurate records.

"So you want me to steal his folder from Guevara's office?"

"I can't hear you when you use certain words. Just get that file."

He hung up. I stared quietly at the wall before I let out a loud "yes." I had taped that phone call. "Holy shit," I yelled. This was too much like a bad movie.

Although Parkman had convinced the State he was clean, this absolutely irrational request to steal Seth's file justified our concern for the boy's safety. Our School Superintendent, well-educated and conversant with education law, asked me to steal a student's record. It felt like a psychological maze as Parkman's behavior spiraled further into irrationality.

The next day, I called Detective Robinson and told him Parkman requested I steal Seth's file. I asked Robinson to come to the school. I played the tape of Parkman's phone call. Robinson asked for the tape and I gave it to him as evidence. I had made two other copies, one for the District Attorney, the other for me.

I didn't sleep the next two nights because my Superintendent asked me to steal a student file. Nobody would believe this had I not taped the call.

Despite all that happened to convince us that Parkman had emotionally impacted Seth, none of us had any proof there was sex. Only Parkman's and Seth's behavior indicated that sex-abuse had happened, and this was totally an inference on our part.

I felt nauseous for several days and nights. None of the authorities could free Seth who continued to defend Parkman. Seth was frightened to do otherwise. Although most of my Cabinet was on vacation, I summoned them to an emergency Cabinet meeting. I needed to be with them rather than go crazy, alone at home, after Parkman's request.

It was a typical hot Clearwater day. The school was empty. Summer School had ended. Football practice had not started. We had the building to ourselves.

By the time we met, I felt less crazed about Parkman's call. I decided to play cute with the information. My Cabinet sat around my conference table, waiting for me to explain why I interrupted their summer vacations. They knew I wouldn't waste their time, but they all had families home, involved in summer fun.

"Parkman called me about 48 hours ago."

They suddenly lost any bad feelings about coming to school on a vacation day. Their hearts collectively stopped. Everything seemed to go into slow motion. I could see they thought I was going to tell them he fired me.

"He asked me if I had keys to Guevara's office and to Guevara's file cabinet." Their eyes opened wider. I went to the point.

"He asked me to steal Seth's file from Guevara's office."

I looked around the table at each face. All were like stone.

"I taped the call."

They screamed and yelled and high-fived.

"That fucking bastard will rot in hell," said Christopher, never at a loss for words even if she looked like a nun.

"You got that right," added Grey.

"Way to go, boss," yelled Nelson.

We were practically dancing.

I sent them to their offices to search their files related to Seth. Although each Assistant Principal supervised an assigned cadre of students based on alphabet, Seth had presented so many incidents that every administrator had a file of their contacts with him. I wanted to consolidate and protect those records.

Carlos Grey was first to return. He opened my door slowly and snaked in as if he were clowning about a mystery movie. Carlos had such a wry sense of humor that I could never tell if he was joking.

"My entire discipline folder on Seth has been stolen!"

I knew he was not faking. He was frightened.

"We're dealing with a lunatic, a fucking maniac," he said.

We just sat there and stared, not knowing what to do. Nelson and Christopher returned and were also stunned by Grey's discovery.

Parkman or somebody had gone into Assistant Principal Grey's locked office and locked cabinet that held 600 students' discipline records. Only one student's discipline folder was stolen. Fortunately, we were able to recreate the entire file from duplicates in Seth's guidance counselor's folder. Whoever did the deed was unaware of the duplicates.

I called Guevara and told him Parkman asked me to steal his files. He came in the following day to duplicate Seth's entire record, lest Parkman or somebody steal that, as well.

CHAPTER 25

Seth's first semester at Bedford High was better for him but not better for me. Parkman became more public with his attacks. He badmouthed me to parents, hoping they'd rebel against me.

From September through December, the battles with Parkman and his Cabinet were constant. We were able to handle the onslaught of demands from his office because we no longer spent time protecting Seth. Parkman's Cabinet started an inquest including sudden requests for my petty cash receipts and a sudden inspection of our attendance records. As these "investigations" continued, we held onto our hope that Parkman would crack under his personal stress or that Seth would disclose.

With Seth at Bedford, beyond his control, Parkman's constant panic and depression made him incapable of running a school district. Seth was now in charge of his own development and his daily routines. Nobody was in charge of the school district and nobody wanted the helm while the leader was having a meltdown. Early evening, on January 8th, with Seth now attending Bedford High for a comfortable half-year, I received a phone call from a familiar voice, a member of the Clearwater Police Department.

"The eagle has been sighted. We have information that will wrap up your concerns of the past year."

The caller hung up.

Ten minutes later, my phone rang again; this time a different voice, another Clearwater cop.

"Mr. Cohen, we just want you to know that we are about to snare your prey." He hung up. I felt giddy.

Ten minutes later, a third call came from yet another cop.

"Don't ask who I am. I just want you to know that we are wiretapping calls from the Superintendent to Seth and expect to have an arrest within hours." After these calls, I knew Lieutenant Somerset was correct in not filing incident reports 18 months earlier. Parkman would never have been caught had reports been filed.

An hour later, a fourth call came. It was the first cop again.

"Hey, you'll be very happy to know that I'm sitting in my patrol car waiting to bust Parkman as a result of telephone tapes." A quick hang-up followed. I wanted to drive to Clearwater but I had a drink instead, maybe two or three.

Ten minutes later, the final call of the evening.

"Mr. Cohen, guess who we have in handcuffs?"

"Really? Thank God it's over."

Seth had finally grown strong enough to emotionally separate from Parkman as a result of being "sheltered" at Bedford High. Without Parkman's daily control, Seth regained his sense of propriety, and disclosed their sexual relationship to his Bedford counselor. She immediately called Child Protection Service who informed her to call the State Police. The State Police switched her call to the Clearwater Police. She met with Somerset and Robinson to share

Seth's disclosure, after which Seth disclosed everything to a police recorder.

With Seth's statement in hand, Robinson met with Judge Fredericks and received permission to tape Seth's calls to Parkman. Seth agreed to discuss past sexual activity with Parkman. Official reports would finally be filed.

Clearwater Mayor, Joe Stevens, was Parkman's neighbor. After hearing sirens, the Mayor looked from his living room window and saw dozens of flashing police lights up the street at Parkman's house.

"Looks like somebody got shot," said the mayor's wife, thinking the worst-case scenario because of the drama created by the red and blue police lights in the dark.

"What's going on," shouted the Mayor, out of breath, as he ran toward the Superintendent's home.

"Just arrested the School Superintendent on child sex abuse charges," answered Lieutenant Foster.

"How come I didn't know anything," screamed the mayor above the din of activity.

"Just found out today when the boy told us about having sex with Parkman."

"A boy? Have we been investigating?"

Questions about the two-year investigation of Parkman were referred to Lieutenant Somerset who had to spend months explaining why he avoided filing any reports prior to Seth's disclosure. Twice, he testified that he feared Parkman would learn of any incident reports.

"Cops are married to teachers. Nothing is secret in Clearwater." It was true that several High School faculty and staff had close family members who were either local police officers or secretaries at the police station. Somerset took heat about the lack of early written reports. His superiors hassled him enough about avoiding incident reports that he retired well before he'd planned.

The search of Parkman's home was completed quickly. Trucks were filled with computers and files while yellow crime-scene tape surrounded the house. Parkman's wife refused to pay his $25,000 bail. She and daughter moved away that night, staying with relatives in New Jersey.

Tenth grader Seth had made the most important decision of his young life. His tumultuous existence could now stabilize.

It had taken us over 18 months from Seth's entry into high school to save him from a controlling deviant whose life as a caring educator covered up his pedophilia. Parkman was arrested, pled guilty to avoid a public trial, and was sentenced to five years.

With Parkman in jail and Seth safely harbored at Bedford, my Cabinet and I could more easily defend ourselves against Parkman's henchmen. They wanted to destroy us before we testified at Grand Jury regarding their knowledge and failure to act. We had barely celebrated victory over Parkman when it became clear that the battles waged by him would be continued by others.

Parkman was in jail.

Seth was safe.

I was not safe.

PART II

CHAPTER 26

The Superintendent's arrest was shocking, even to those who had harbored thoughts of Parkman abusing Seth. After Clearwater citizens accepted the jailing of their School Superintendent, the Orange County District Attorney began investigating "who knew what when." He wanted to know if other District leaders were criminally negligent by their lack of intervention and their silence.

A grand jury was convened to determine if any indictments for complacency should be served. School Board members were first to testify, after which Board President Fletcher publicly denied any knowledge of anybody's concerns about Parkman.

"None were brought to me," he told newspaper reporters. I knew he was wrong because I had gone to him and he had admitted to me that I wasn't the first to bring the relationship to his attention.

Although I couldn't debate him publicly about this, Fletcher's early awareness of Parkman and Seth was exposed when a local newspaper published the actual "warning" letter from Fletcher. That letter was dated months before Parkman's arrest. So, he knew and subsequently admitted under oath that he'd been warned of the relationship by several educators and parents. The warning letter had been written when Dr. Guevara and Seth's teachers threatened to go public with their concerns.

Several board members were re-called to Grand Jury after conflicting testimonies were given about their knowledge of Parkman's relationship with Seth. Board members eventually agreed that I and others had expressed concerns to them, but Fletcher told reporters "school board members had no responsibility for overseeing the Superintendent and, therefore, had no responsibility for reporting his personal behavior or misdeeds even if concerns about the relationship had been expressed to them." This caused a public outcry which resulted in the ousting of Fletcher and several other Board members at the next election.

Parkman's friends continued attempts to undermine my school leadership after his jailing. They occupied my time with new reporting requirements aimed at making me a less-effective leader. I was constantly putting out fires lit by the jailed child-molester's friends. I had "hands-on" support from my assistant principals and several teachers, all of whom were eventually punished for helping me meet the constant demands for unnecessary information. They lost their leadership titles such as "Department Chairperson" or "Wrestling Coach," along with the additional money they earned from these responsibilities.

The business community blindly supported Board President Fletcher. One local businessman withdrew his pledge to carpet our new Computer Academy. This delayed the technology installation and student instruction by months. School District leadership and the business leaders were all concerned about my upcoming Grand Jury testimony. If they could undermine my reputation, I'd be a less credible witness. Their contrived complaints about our school grew so pervasive that an assistant district attorney learned of it and privately warned me, "A handful of locals and several of their friends in the School District are out to destroy you."

The resulting Grand Jury Report about "who knew what when," exposed those who knew about Parkman's relationship with Seth but failed to give names. It used words like "Supervisor" and "Assistant." The report did make clear that I, "the High School Principal," was the only administrator who reported concerns to the police. On seeing this in local papers, the shocked business community stopped their attacks on me and no longer supported the Board. Local politicians called for a cease fire between the School District and me.

With Parkman in prison, reporters wrote that "many people had seen Seth with Parkman enough times to have been concerned." The newspaper emphasized that I was the only administrator to have reported concerns to police and other authorities. When this was published, several of Parkman's former Cabinet Members told me I "should not have reported Parkman because I had no evidence." Even after he confessed and was jailed, several of his staff refused to believe he abused the boy. They blamed me for "starting a process that caused his guilt."

Prison sign-in books secured under Freedom of Information, show members of Parkman's Cabinet visiting the now-sentenced child-molester in prison. With Parkman's help from prison, they continued his plan to fire me but now had their own reasons. These Cabinet members knew I would tell Grand Jury I had gone to them with my concerns. They had to take severe action against me prior to my testimony.

At 7:00 a.m. Monday morning, two months after Parkman's arrest and jailing, Interim Superintendent Donald Ross was waiting in my office when I arrived. Ross knew I told the Grand Jury I went to him with my concerns about Parkman. He knew this because I had already told local newspapers I'd gone to Ross and others for help in stopping Parkman.

Ross yelled with a trembling voice.

"I have a letter of complaint, Mr. Cohen that warrants our immediate action." I interrupted him immediately.

"Please say nothing more until I bring in a witness." I summoned Assistant Principal Nelson to my office and told him, "The Interim Superintendent has informed me he is about to state complaints about me. I need you here as a witness." He acknowledged Ross and stood fast.

Ross continued, "I received an anonymous letter and I want to meet with the entire high school staff to inform them of an investigation I am about to conduct as a follow-up to anonymous complaints."

I was stunned. There had been no prior discussion about any complaints against me. Preliminary talks were required by my union's contract, had a complaint, in fact, been lodged.

I had anticipated Parkman's Cabinet would take some kind of quick action against me. To protect myself, I hired a private attorney, Chris Watkins. I told Chris that certain district staff had ignored my concerns about Parkman and would need to ruin my credibility in order to undermine my testimony against them. I did not expect to need Chris this soon. Ross was moving fast. At 7:00 a.m. it was too early to call Chris. I was on my own. Ross continued.

"I have a letter in my hand with complaints warranting a thorough investigation of you. I want you to immediately call the entire staff to a meeting in the library where I will let them know about these allegations and advise them of my investigation because I will be calling teachers in for interviews about the charges."

I refused to announce an immediate staff meeting. I was not going to let him bulldoze me, especially when I knew his motives were aimed at destroying me.

"I will not call the staff together unless you tell me the charges you have against me." By now, the new Board President, Theresa Bradley, and the District's Business Manager, entered my office. They had arrived earlier with Ross and seven others in a well-planned military-styled takeover of the building.

Fortunately, I was not caught off-guard because Nelson secretly telephoned me while I was driving to work.

"Boss, the marines have landed. Ross came in five minutes ago with seven others. They each had an assignment to take over part of the school after Ross proclaimed he was now in charge of the building."

Nelson was out of breath from running up six flights of stairs to a room where he could call me without being noticed.

"One of Ross' gang ran to the counseling office and told people an investigation was underway and they could not touch any files. Another of his cronies ran to the Attendance Office and told that group the same thing."

Nelson described an organized platoon led by Ross, a former Navy officer. The mission was aimed at securing records, as if a crime had been committed.

I was 20 minutes from school when Nelson called. I had time to think. I knew Parkman's friends wanted me dead but, perhaps, we could negotiate a deal. Should I make-believe I'm surprised to see them? Should I turn around and call in sick? I could not rely on Ross being rational. He and others feared my testimony as viscerally as Parkman feared Seth's testimony. I felt strength in having truth as my weapon but I was powerless in the path of their lies and attacks.

From notes taken by police and the District's lawyer during interviews of key District Staff, we later learned that every time I went to Ross to express my concerns about Parkman, he immediately told Parkman all I had said. The courts provided these notes to my attorney. We were shocked. We expected better from a former Navy officer, but Ross thought I was lying and was after Parkman's job. Now, in taking over my school, he seemed nervous, unsure he was doing the right thing.

"You do not intimidate me, Mr. Cohen, and I will do what I want to do, not what you tell me to do."

Ross stood on his toes to accentuate his 6'4" height but he was trembling. I sensed he knew he was doing wrong. This take-over could not have been Board-approved. Yet, it was happening with the involvement of the new Board President, Fletcher's Vice President.

I looked Ross in the eye and thought about the truth.

"In front of your witnesses I will tell you that I refuse to call a staff meeting unless you tell me what charges are contained in that letter." I gave no ground. I knew the entire staff had to be buzzing about this invasion. I took strength from their support.

"I know my rights as Superintendent," Ross screamed. He slammed my office door so nobody would hear him yelling. He had not expected any resistance from me. So, I gave him more.

"I've taken twice as many law courses as you. So, with no disrespect, unless you tell me what those complaints are, I know I can refuse to allow any staff meeting to take place."

I knew I had a right to hear the complaints he was planning to announce and he knew, as well, because he then read the letter aloud. ". . . charges of intimidating staff . . . charges of stealing petty cash . . . charges of changing test scores for favors . . . charges of creating a hostile work environment . . ." and so on.

I smiled over at Nelson and he smiled back. We had expected to hear some phony sexual charges to make me appear to be another Parkman. I was actually relieved by these charges. "Sure, I'll call a staff meeting."

I went to the P.A. system and announced "a brief but urgent meeting of all teaching and clerical staff." I kept security on post because students were already entering the building for first period classes.

Within minutes, there were 150 teachers and other staff packed into the school library. They knew via the grapevine that Ross had taken over the building. I turned on a small tape recorder, placed it on a nearby library table and greeted the gathering, "Good Morning. Mr. Ross has an announcement to make."

With that, Ross read aloud charges as they had purportedly been presented in an anonymous letter. While Ross was reading the charges for all to hear, the District's Personnel Director and the new Board President tried to stop him. They knew he was violating my personnel rights by publicly announcing anonymously written charges against me. Ross continued the letter-reading, ignoring the attempts to interrupt him.

When he finished reading the charges, the teachers rebelled. Several yelled out.

"You're pressing charges based on an anonymous letter . . . what if somebody gave you anonymous charges about me," the photography teacher said, "Would you immediately start an investigation and announce it publicly . . . whatever happened to personnel rights . . ."

The meeting abruptly ended because so many teachers were angered and outspoken. Ross lost control of the rebellious crowd and dismissed them.

Thus began a nine-month daily "investigation" of every check I signed, every letter I wrote, every test I scored, every requisition I approved, all trip reports I authorized, interviews I conducted, teacher observations I wrote, parent letters I composed, payroll records I authorized and every other aspect of a high school principal's daily work. It was more than tedious. It was emotionally overwhelming.

CHAPTER 27

I could trust about 95 percent of the 250 high school staff. The hard-line detractors were those I had removed from chairman positions when I arrived in Clearwater or were teachers to whom I had given negative evaluations I did not expect their support.

These disgruntled staff were the first to be interviewed by Ross' investigators after the library meeting. When I complained to local media about the stacked-deck of hostile witnesses, several neutral interviewees were added to Ross' investigation. All these teachers hostile or otherwise, expected to be interviewed about the charges Ross read aloud in the library. Instead, most of the interview questions addressed Parkman's visits to Seth at the High School and my reaction to his visits, implying by question, that I did not report my concerns to the District.

Even the detractors on my staff were nervous when it became known that questioning focused on the Parkman issue. Would they be implicating themselves if they admit they witnessed Parkman's visits and did not file any reports? The questions asked were aimed at implicating me, but teachers worried because they were also mandated reporters with a legal obligation to report potential sex abuse.

To build their case against me, the District hired Special Attorney, Jacques Concorde, "to investigate who knew what when."

A memo was issued to all staff about Concorde's role and the upcoming District Attorney investigation. The memo directed staff to inform the Acting Superintendent "if you are summoned to testify at Grand Jury." When my assistants and I informed Ross that we'd been summoned, he directed us to be interviewed by Concorde prior to Grand Jury. Ross told us that Concorde would advise us, "to ensure we told the truth." It was clear to me that Concorde wanted to know what we would tell the Grand Jury so he could assist Fletcher and Ross with their Grand Jury testimony. Our union lawyer counseled us to meet with Concorde. "You'll be charged with insubordination if you do not answer Concorde's questions."

"Bullshit!" I told my Cabinet. "I'll not speak with Concorde just so he knows what I'm going to say! He's not my lawyer. That's confidential!"

My attorney, Chris Watkins, told the District and local media that he'd not allow Concorde to question me because I was in conflict with the District's stance on the Parkman case. I told my Cabinet they could legally do the same.

Watkins explained that my knowledge was in direct conflict-of-interest with public statements made by District leadership who still maintained that no suspicions of Parkman wrongdoing had been brought to their attention. By now, nearly all the teachers and community leaders knew I'd gone to the police and to the Board about Parkman. When the District leadership publicly stated that nobody had come to them, a legal conflict between me and them was created.

I refused to tell my supervisors or Concorde what I planned to tell the Grand Jury. I refused to be interviewed. Nelson also refused to be interviewed. We ignored the advice of our union lawyer who wanted us to tell Concorde everything. Instead of going to Concorde, I went unannounced to the District Attorney's office.

D.A. Francis was shocked when I showed up and told him about Concorde's "investigation" and attempts to pry information from us before we went to his Grand Jury. Francis immediately held a press conference about Concorde, suggesting the "possibility of witness tampering and/or interference with justice." The District's investigation abruptly ended. Concorde quit but the District hired attorneys Barbara Paris and Lenny Dickson to continue investigating me on charges that were designed by the now-jailed Parkman.

Assistant D.A. Hoovler interviewed me in his office for many hours on several occasions. He seemed to be building a case of complicity against certain individuals who expressed knowledge of Parkman's obsession but did nothing. Hoovler confirmed with Clearwater Police that I'd reported to them two years earlier and that they asked me to put nothing in writing. The police also confirmed that nobody else had reported to them other than anonymous callers.

Chris Watkins' words became a mantra and remained clear in my mind as Grand Jury time approached. "You want disclosure. You really want disclosure. You want the Grand Jury to know everything. Tell them everything that you ever thought about Parkman regarding this case. Tell them about everybody you went to for help. Let them know about all those with whom you shared your concerns about Parkman. Full disclosure is best for everybody."

It was frightening to think about telling the grand jurors about all those from whom we sought help in keeping Parkman away from Seth. Would they believe we reached out to so many and that nobody could help? Parkman had become so adept at Jekyll, that nobody questioned Hyde. No matter what evidence people saw in Parkman's behavior, they refused to believe the worst was possible.

I was not frightened when Ross came in with a "platoon" to take over the school. I was not frightened when I confronted my boss about his obsession. I wasn't even frightened when I went to the police or even when I spoke with Parkman's family. Very little about this case had frightened me. I had always been calmed by knowing I was doing right. I had faith in the system. I believed. But, on the first day of Grand Jury testimony, I awoke in a cold sweat.

Horrible scenarios were popping into my head. What if the Grand Jury thinks I knew Parkman was having sex? What if the Grand Jury thinks I actually helped him? What if the Grand Jury thinks I covered up for Parkman? I should have filled out police forms despite their urgings to do otherwise. I should have pushed my supervisors into action. I should have wrestled Parkman to the ground in front of the school when he came to visit Seth. I should have stood on top of the school building, yelling that I suspect our Superintendent is a pervert, sexually involved with a child!!!

I showered, dressed, and left for the hour drive to Grand Jury in Goshen, New York. It was a beautiful, sunny day outside, but inside me was cold and shivery.

As I was driving on the New York State Thruway where it turns north at Suffern, a huge bald eagle glided 30 yards directly over my car. The sunroof was open. I watched him pass overhead, close enough for me to wave through the open roof and imagine I got a wing lift indicating he saw me. I pulled over to the side of the road to watch it make a wide circle and land on a tree a quarter mile away. The eagle was a good sign. Now I was relaxed and ready for Grand Jury. The rest of the drive was beautiful, inside and out.

I lost a bit of that calm when I entered the Courthouse and was immediately swept by armed guards into the Grand Jury room to avoid contact with people in the waiting area. It was a small, steep theater. I was seated on a low stage with the Jury Foreman. The Grand Jury was in the audience. There were 22 of them spread around 50 seats.

I was interviewed by two District attorneys who stood between the jury and the stage. Two other D.A.s periodically added questions from the sidelines. Their queries included every aspect of my relationship with Parkman and the observations and reports I made to District leaders and other authorities. My testimony took 14 hours over two days of intense, often devious questions, aimed at determining if criminal charges should be filed against any of those to whom I reported my concerns.

After the first three hours of testimony, the District Attorney called a ten minute recess. Jurors were told they could not speak with me during the break. I was directed to speak with nobody because I was still under oath. I was brought to a nearby waiting room.

As soon as my escort left me, I was immediately confronted by Jacques Concorde who ran into the room and spoke in rapid fire.

"Okay, we stopped our investigation, but I need to speak with you. I'm now hired by the District just to speak with you, not speak to others about you. I have been trying to speak with you for weeks.

You have not returned my phone calls. I am considered a higher level district employee and you must respond to me. I want to discuss this case with you. You will be insubordinate if you do not co-operate with me."

Here I was, on a ten-minute break after hours of difficult, emotional testimony and now Concorde was making the scene even more stressful.

"Do you know that I am right now sworn in and giving Grand Jury testimony?"

"I don't need to speak with you now. You don't have to answer me now. I just want you to know that I must speak with you tomorrow or the next day. I need to speak with you right away." Without answering, I turned and walked away.

A few minutes later, the jury foreman summoned me. I took the stand. The District Attorney asked me if I was ready to continue testimony.

"I am not ready to continue testimony because I was just confronted by the School District lawyer, Jacques Concorde." I then described the conversation. The District Attorney said he'd communicate with the School District and Mr. Concorde. They gave me a few more minutes to relax before we started.

At the close of my second full day of testimony, I was walking to my car in the courthouse parking lot when I heard a low voice behind me.

"Please don't turn around." I was frightened.

"We Grand Jury members are not supposed to speak with any witnesses, but I want to tell you that I'm glad you're Principal of that High School because my daughter will be there in two years and I'm pleased about how you tried to protect the boy."

Impulsively, I started turning around, but I felt a hand on my back and the juror again asked me not to see his face. At that point another voice spoke.

"I'm also a juror. I have no children. But, I live in Clearwater and I went to Clearwater High School and I am very proud that you are our high school's principal. You did everything possible. The only other thing you might have done is beat him up at the front door and then you'd be in jail with him."

I went directly to my car. I sat there, stunned, for ten minutes before I could drive.

I was one of the last to testify about "who knew what when." School board members, Assistant Superintendents and other District authorities had already been questioned. At the end of my testimony, I was told that I contradicted the testimony of others and I was asked if I wanted to review and possibly change certain responses. I asked for a review but changed none of my responses. The Assistant District Attorney then advised me they'd call in those whose responses differed from mine unless I changed my answers. I was also told that I'd be re-called if those I contradicted didn't change their responses. I changed nothing.

The District Attorney's office seemed strong when they re-called witnesses who did, in fact change their testimony after hearing my words read aloud to them. But, nobody was indicted. The D.A. felt it was not his role to provide the State Education Department with the names of those who failed to report concerns about Parkman. Although the Grand Jury Report stated that "The High School Principal was the only administrator to express concerns to police," no charges were filed as a result of the D.A.'s investigation into "who knew what when."

I was now in bigger trouble because the Grand Jury Report did not protect me from retaliation. The D.A. did not punish those on whom he initially set his sights. As such, anyone I implicated for knowing about Seth and Parkman could now attack me because they had essentially beaten the charges.

Acting Superintendent Ross and Board President Fletcher publicly criticized the District Attorney's Grand Jury Report. They re-implemented the District's own investigation into "who knew what when," questioning more High School staff about my knowledge of the relationship.

Again, investigators interviewed teachers who had a grudge against me. One long-married ex-Chair told investigators that she heard me say, "I knew Parkman was in the boy's pants." She lied and also neglected to tell investigators I had earlier criticized her for having an inappropriate relationship with a teacher under her supervision. Disgruntled staff were now the only voices sought by Ross' investigators.

Another Chairperson I demoted told several teachers, "I could retire but I'm going to stay here until I destroy Cohen any way I can." He was the first to be interviewed.

With Grand Jury completed, the School District's investigation did not interfere with justice, and could not be stopped by the District Attorney as he'd done earlier. I was summoned to be interviewed by the district lawyers, Paris and Dickson and had no option but to comply. Additional charges were added at the interview.

"After we began investigating the initial four charges, we had a right to collect any and all information regarding Mr. Cohen's performance."

The School District had three attorneys present to interrogate me about my knowledge of Parkman. I had one attorney.

Their questions about Parkman seemed designed to protect those to whom I had directly brought my concerns. When they asked about my first awareness of Parkman's involvement with Seth, I told them about the telephone calls we received from Seth's teachers while Seth was still in middle school. I told them about my direct confrontation with Parkman as well as my outreach to others. I felt like they were frustrated by my full disclosure. I was actually giving them information about Parkman they'd not had, including our monitoring of Parkman. With nothing to hide about Parkman, there was nothing for them to uncover. So, they began focusing on non-Parkman matters, particularly on the changing of State test scores for nine specific recent graduates.

The test issue started three years earlier when I had a heart-to-heart talk with the High School Science Chairperson, Tony Scozzafava. He came to my office to ask if I was planning to continue his wife as softball coach. He had heard rumors that players, parents and others were unhappy about her coaching. In the opinion of other coaches, Rosalie Scozzafava had failed as varsity softball coach. My decision to replace her was not about her team's won and loss record. It was about her poor organization of practice sessions, her inability to motivate players, and the continuous complaints from parents about her leadership style. Girls had been quitting the team in anger for several years.

"I'm discussing this with you because you asked and because I know how important this High School is to you, Tony," I told him. "I'm not selecting your wife as softball coach for next season. I've been to practice sessions with Assistant Principal Nelson who was also a coach and I've been to the games. I'm pretty sure your wife is going to be happier when she's not responsible for the girls' softball program. She sure doesn't seem happy when she's coaching."

Scozzafava agreed. In fact, he gave several additional reasons for her to give up coaching.

"She's never home during the season. The money is less important than her health. This will be a good thing you're doing for her."

Months later, during the administration of the annual State science tests, Scozzafava came to my office for the first time since our meeting about his wife. Though he'd been quite understanding at the time, I later heard he was negative about me since I replaced her. I was cautious. He announced his reason for being there.

"You always tell us to bring State tests to you for seniors who need the test to graduate but failed by only one or two points."

I was really too busy at that moment and explained my situation.

"Got Nelson here working on tomorrow's graduation ceremonies. Got Norris here because we've got a security issue in process. Got the police on the phone to discuss graduation logistics. So, I hope we can deal with this quickly."

Scozzafava explained he had 20 twelfth graders who would not graduate because they failed the State Science exam by only one or two points. It has long been a practice among high school principals to personally review State exams of any senior who would not graduate because of one or two test points. This ensures that no child misses graduation because of a scoring error.

We sat and reviewed the tests while the room buzzed with graduation preparation, including loud parents who were irate because their children were not graduating. We focused on test items that had received a score of zero to see if an additional point should be awarded.

A point was found for nine of the 20 students. In each case, I crossed out the total score and raised it to a score of 65, putting my initials on each of the changed total scores and allowing the child to graduate.

I was also required to initial the changed test item in addition to the changed total score but I forgot and only signed each child's changed total score. Of the ten thousand tests reviewed by the District during this investigation, only these nine showed a "technical error" where I had forgotten to initial the changed item.

I'm convinced that Scozzafava noticed I had only initialed the totals. One of his teachers told me that he returned to the scoring room, saying, "I think I'll use these tests to teach our principal a lesson." At the time, I'd not a clue to what that could've meant.

Three years later, in the interrogation room, the District lawyers handed me each of the nine tests. They questioned me about the absence of initials on changed items. I admitted my mistake in signing the total scores but failing to initial each changed item. They would not accept my signature on each total score as proof that I was not trying to hide changed scores.

"We can only deal with facts, not causality," they glibly stated.

Chapter 28

"Here are some other questions that are also based in fact," Paris went on. "Did you order six computers from one of your school budgets rather than the District's technology budget?"

"Yes. There was never anything wrong with those orders. All our schools order some of their own equipment in addition to what the District buys for us."

"Did you purchase 15 Palm Pilots with one of your school budgets?"

"Yes."

Paris then shocked me with an accusation that had never occurred to me when I had earlier predicted how vicious she'd get.

"We think those items are missing. We want to see those items right now. We'll go to the school so you can show them to us immediately." It sounded like a setup.

I looked at my lawyer and said, "What if somebody stole them?"

I saw a momentary look of panic on Chris' face. He whispered in my ear.

"Is there anything we need to be worrying about here, something I should know?"

"No," I answered, "Except that people do steal things and if somebody told Paris that items were missing and never told me . . ."

Watkins and I drove to my office in my car while the attorneys drove close behind. We arrived simultaneously. It was obvious they wanted me to have no time in my office without them.

"The first thing I need to see," Paris barked, "are the 15 Palm Pilots."

I'd already distributed one of the Palms to the English Department Chairperson who just happened to be standing outside my office at that moment.

"Would you like to see Mr. Richards' Palm Pilot or would you like to see the other 14?" She wanted to see the other 14. She was impatient.

"Richards already informed us about receiving one." He may have also told them I'd stolen the others since they had not yet been distributed. Richards was not a supporter.

"Let's see them right now," Paris demanded.

"You want to see them right now? I used sarcasm to keep myself grounded rather than join her high pressure pace.

"Yes."

I saw another nervous look on my lawyer's face. So, I brought him into my own sense of calm.

"You getting all this," I asked him. He smiled.

I turned to Paris.

"If I open this closet door and the Palm Pilots are not there, I'm going to call the police right now to report stolen Palm Pilots and I'll tell the police you knew they were stolen but I did not."

I could tell from her body language she knew I was serious. She fidgeted. I took out my keys, found the key to that closet and opened it. On the eye-level shelf was a small carton with all the Palm Pilots.

"You want to count them," I asked sarcastically.

"Yes."

Suddenly it was difficult to control my anger. My hands clenched. I stood at the closet; staring at Paris as she stood in my doorway looking like she wanted to run away after failing to discover the Palms missing. But, she held her ground.

Still standing uncomfortably in the doorway rather than entering my office, Paris, more subdued, continued. "I also need to ask you where three computers are. Three computers that you ordered and nobody knows where they are." There was only one person, a bookkeeper, who had access to that data.

"The clerk who told you these items are missing has a grudge and you fell for it." My anger burst out. "I told that clerk she'd have to share her overtime hours next year and she went into a crazy rage on me."

Several months earlier, that clerk had exploded with a temper I'd not seen from any school employee in my decades of supervisory experience. The depravity of her vulgarity demonstrated she'd stop at nothing to keep her overtime hours, including falsifying charges against me.

"I'd eat shit off the floor for my children, but I won't eat shit off the floor to keep this job. You do what you need to do, and I'll do what I need to do," she warned, while trying to intimidate me with a pointed finger in my face.

I then telephoned the Assistant Personnel Director, Karen King, who asked me not to write her up. "The woman has serious emotional issues", King said, "and I'd rather speak with her personally about the manner in which she addressed you."

The false accusation about "missing" computer equipment was eventually linked to that clerk. She also falsely reported to Paris that I had been paid for overtime hours I never worked. This last accusation took many days to disprove because I had to account for my overtime presence on each day she claimed I did not work overtime. Neither she nor others were charged with making false reports about me after I proved their charges wrong.

During the months after Parkman's arrest, the half-dozen remaining "Bernie Bashers" kept feeding the bloodthirsty investigators with leads to my potential missteps. This would lead to more charges and further investigation. Fourteen charges were eventually listed by the investigators in their attempt to discredit my Grand Jury testimony. They eventually dropped all charges related to stealing money, stealing equipment, intimidating personnel, creating a hostile work environment, inflating student scores in return for favors and other lesser charges that were never even investigated. The public was informed about all the initial charges but never was told about the dropped charges.

The technical charge regarding my signature on the State tests gave the investigators the legal grip they sought. Their Parkman-related charges were weak because of the Grand Jury Report and newspaper reports. They needed this test technicality to generate legal action against me.

The resolve and fierceness of the investigators convinced me they'd suspend me from my job to make me appear guilty while they continued their investigation. Evidence of our school's attempts to stop Parkman was strong. The investigators could not contend with my presence at the school on a day-to-day basis because teachers were beginning to loudly complain about the investigation's insincerity and intrusiveness into our school's operations. Parents were also protesting. The investigators thought I organized all the protests. I didn't. Teachers, parents and students organized protests on their own with no involvement from me. They spoke at School Board meetings and gave media interviews about the investigation's intrusiveness into our school's functioning.

I told Assistant Principal Nelson and Security Chief Norris that my suspension was imminent. They helped me pack my many personal belongings and sneak them out into my car after dark. I sensed Ross would not suspend me in a humane manner. I wanted my personal belongings out of there.

We packed over a dozen cartons with my personal books, cameras, lenses, medications, extra clothing, coffee maker, laptop, professional journals, baseball cleats, awards, my own high school football and wrestling letters, and many other personal items I had in my office from a long career. We took down large framed photos from my travels to Asia and the Amazon Rainforest. Previously cluttered walls were now bare. Nobody asked why.

Two days after we emptied out most of my personal items, making the large office seem empty, the Interim Superintendent telephoned.

"Bern, I need you to come over to my office right now. We have something very important to discuss."

"Right now," I questioned, facetiously.

"Right now."

I took a long look around my office. I told my secretaries I was called to meet with the boss and did not expect to be back. They gave me a puzzled look.

"I believe he's calling me over to suspend me while they continue their investigation."

"No, he would never do that . . . people will not allow it to happen . . .," they pleaded, supportively.

Unbeknownst to me, three of Ross' henchmen watched me drive away from the school, after which they ran into my office with a big role of yellow emergency, police-type, crime-scene tape. They taped the drawers of my file cabinets and my desk so nothing could be removed.

When I took my personal belongings from the office, I purposely completely emptied the desk drawers. All drawers were bare. I wanted them to be shocked at finding a totally empty desk. What went through their minds when they pulled open drawer after drawer and found a perfectly clean, empty desk, not even a paper clip?

"Did he ever work at his desk . . . did he know we were coming . . . how could he have known we were coming . . . who has a desk with absolutely nothing in it . . .did somebody ignore the crime scene tape and steal his stuff?"

I laugh every time I imagine Ross, Paris and Concorde dramatically cutting open the crime-scene tape to find all drawers bare, a totally empty desk. I wanted to put a note in the desk, "Fuck you, I figured you were coming," but I refrained.

I waited outside the boss' office until he got the "all-clear" from the crime-scene posse. He called me in.

"The Board of Education has directed me to assign you to your home for the remainder of this investigation. I know this will be difficult for the school, but I have no choice. You will work at home until the investigation is complete and I will give you work assignments." He also told me not to return to my school except to get my car. I told him this was not necessary. I drove home. Tears streamed down my face.

I cried for my school and students as I drove. I knew I'd done right. I thought I'd eventually win the war, perhaps, easier fought from a position off the battlefield. I could now fight on a full-time basis and have them paying me while I fight. Ironic. But, painful.

CHAPTER 29

Ross assigned me a series of research projects. He had me conduct a study of New York school districts' success with certain curricula. To complete the research, I requested a district laptop and a telephone. The District was cooperative. "Come by the district office Monday and we'll give you a cell phone and laptop to be used only for this research."

After I picked up the laptop and cell phone, I went to my car, turned on the cell phone, and saw "GPS" flash on the screen for a nano-second as the phone booted. At that time, 2003, only high-end cell phones had a GPS. School district phones did not include such costly features. I called Verizon to ask if that particular phone model came equipped with a GPS.

"No, not unless it is installed as a special item."

"Can you tell me, please, if my phone has a GPS specially installed?"

The Verizon representative was obliging.

"It seems your office asked us to install a GPS locater in your phone, because they want to know where you are in case you're in an accident. It says you don't work in a school, only in the field, and they need to track you. That's what it says here."

When I got home with the phone, I kept it turned on so their tracking device would get a constant signal of my kitchen cabinet. I never took it with me when I left home, except when I brought it to the Spy Store in New York City where they verified that a special GPS locater had been installed. They sold me security shields for the laptop and phone, making them impervious to monitoring. I felt like I'd won a battle. Now I could take the phone and laptop to my boat and enjoy a day on the river while conducting the telephone research. I wondered where else they planted tracking devices.

Following the discovery of the GPS installation, a series of spy attacks on my personal computer were traced back to a nearby university office staffed by a close relative of a School District employee. The spying included keystroke monitoring, allowing them to see every word I typed. I didn't know if they were spying for the imprisoned Parkman or for the "who knew what when" investigation. I reported this to the District Attorney.

I did not live in Clearwater. Attacks on my home computer were under a different law enforcement jurisdiction. The D.A. and police with whom I'd long worked on this case could not help me. They advised me to speak with police where I then lived, in Piermont, New York, but I did not want to attract local media. My life in Piermont, far enough away from Clearwater, had not been impacted by the case. I wanted to keep it that way and decided to leave my name off the local police blotter. For the next year, every time I was on my computer, I had to imagine that somebody could see every keystroke I made. To begin writing this book and other personal documents, I bought a laptop and never connected it to the Internet.

Parkman's trial was months away. In the interim, a District Technology Specialist, Joe Sinopoli, was accused by the police of protecting Parkman by eliminating child porn from the Superintendent's computer. Shortly after this police discovery, several men began taking turns sitting in a pickup truck with radio equipment and headsets, right below my second-floor apartment window. I was afraid to tell anybody about the men because I didn't want people to think I had lost my sanity. I kept my shades drawn and spoke on the phone in whispers to avoid their listening equipment. I did begin to question my sanity. Was the investigation making me paranoid or were those men really monitoring me?

Several days after I noticed the men sitting in the truck for over ten hours a day, Dr. Guevara called. He told me he'd been followed home by two private investigators who sat outside his house in a red pickup truck until he went out and confronted them. My paranoia was replaced by anger. Using a telephoto lens, I photographed the license plate of the truck. A friendly cop ran the plate for me and identified the truck as registered to a private investigation firm in Poughkeepsie, over two hours away.

"Why would they hire somebody local who you might know," police told me when I asked why they'd hire somebody so distant.

The monitoring was constant. It became very bothersome. I stayed away from the windows. Police told me the district could legally monitor my home departures and arrivals during regular school hours because I was officially on their payroll, "assigned to my home." My lawyer told me I was not under house arrest and I could define my own work hours as long as I kept completing my assignments.

After a month, the men in trucks came less frequently. They realized I was sneaking away by parking my car elsewhere. It became a game. I went out during the day and did my assigned work at odd hours of the night. I met their deadlines.

My escape from this madness took the form of stage and film acting. Every high school principal comes from one of the academic disciplines (math, science, etc.). Mine was theater. I took the opportunity of this suspension, to return to professional acting by taking acting classes in New York City. This was a great escape from the caged-up sense of exile.

Although the spies came less frequently, they began showing up at night. My daytime departures apparently gave them a right to be there in the evening. On several evenings, they followed me in their truck when I went out socially. I was now single. My wife and I split during this case. On a date with Carol, I noticed we were being followed. I felt they were hoping to catch me doing something reportable, like a Parkman-type situation. Otherwise, why follow me?

I took a chance and told Carol we were being followed. We had dated enough so I knew she didn't think I was crazy. I made a series of local, meaningless left and right turns to prove to Carol they were following. Then, with Carol listening, I telephoned my sister, Judy, in Maine and described my situation. I trusted Carol but I wanted another witness. Judy stayed on the line for my next maneuver.

I told Carol to hold on tight while I made a sharp U-turn on Piermont's Main Street as I described the action to my sister. Now the spy would be noticed if he did the same. He pulled over and stopped. He did not make a U-turn. I made another U-turn, putting us behind him. My camera's flashbulb lit the night as I photographed his license plate and honked before he finally drove away. The spying stopped, I thought.

CHAPTER 30

It had always been my long-range plan to use retirement as a return to film and stage acting. I had been a professional actor until I was 26 when I decided to take a more active role in parenting my two children; something that acting's schedule did not permit. I left acting and went into education with no regrets and a long-range plan to return.

The suspension from Clearwater was an opportunity to get an earlier return to acting rather than just sit home and weep about my situation. The District's investigation would continue no matter where I spent my days, so I took this opportunity to return to acting several years earlier than expected.

I had no prior training in film acting because it wasn't part of Adelphi University's Theatre Program when I majored in Theater Arts during the Sixties. To upgrade my skills, I interviewed at three New York City acting studios that focused on acting-for-the-camera, and selected Penny Templeton Studio.

I attended three semesters of Penny Templeton's four-hour Monday night on-camera class in which I was old enough to be parent to all the other students. An additional semester studying with Ruth Nerkin at the New York School of Film and Television, gave me the confidence to begin auditioning.

Before testing myself at auditions, I mailed my headshot to director Jonathan Demme (*Silence of the Lambs*) who was then shooting the *Manchurian Candidate*. I had met him because he lives in my neighborhood. I thought he might counsel me or at least speak with me if I wrote him about being a local high school principal nearing retirement, considering a return to acting. I did not mention the Clearwater situation.

I did get a call but not from Demme.

"Hi, this is Tim from casting. Jon Demme wants you to be one of the Manchurian Men in a scene shooting in two days. Can you be there?"

"Sure. Where and what?"

He told me to dress like a billionaire with a dark suit and an upscale tie. Here was my chance to see if this is what I wanted to do. The classes with Penny and Ruth had often been a challenge. They were film acting classes to which I had brought a 30-year-old skillset for stage-acting. Stage techniques and camera techniques are very different, to an embarrassing degree. I learned this the hard way from brutally blunt but patient teachers when I over-acted in film class by using stage techniques.

I bought a new "billionaire" tie and showed up at the Yonkers Studio in a navy pin striped suit, an off-white shirt rather than a bright white shirt (learned that from Penny) and a corporate haircut. I had no lines to speak but I still thought I'd get enough exposure to the environment to see if it was as interesting as stage-acting.

I entered the studio and got in line at a sign-in table. After I signed in, I was told "You're number 19."

"What's that mean," I asked.

After absorbing an eye-roll from the 20-something at the check-in table, I told her this was my first experience. Her attitude changed immediately. I think she then saw me as somebody's grandpa. She took me aside.

"You're a background actor. You stay here in 'holding' until you hear your number called or somebody calls for the Manchurian Men. First, go to wardrobe where they'll approve your costume and send you to makeup."

She was brusque but informative and this, after all, was not a classroom. This was the real deal and I was surrounded by actors, lighting technicians, and the works. I was no longer the high school principal in-charge. I was being told what to do by somebody just a bit older than my students.

In wardrobe, they loved my suit but hated the tie. "Too bold for a real billionaire." They had dozens of ties. They even ironed my suit. I was impressed but I could see their attention to my wardrobe had nothing to do with me. I was an object to them, a piece of the background.

In makeup, it was fun to see them "rich" me up with a tan and a razor cut to my beard. In both places, wardrobe and makeup, I tried to hang around to watch them work on others but I could only stretch my welcome to a point, before I was in the way.

I returned to holding with mixed feelings. "Holding" sounded so barbaric. And, the word "background" seemed more demeaning than "extra." Although I was having fun, I could easily sense that wardrobe and makeup people felt I was only a mannequin for the camera. But, "I'm here," I thought, "I'll stay for the next part." And, the food was very good.

I sat in holding with plenty to do. Penny warned her classes we'd spend most of the day waiting when we worked on a film. She was right. I'd brought my research to keep me busy. Most of the background actors napped, read a book, or chatted jealously about the principal actors. I wrote Clearwater research reports.

Finally, they called for the Manchurian Men. I followed about eight other billionaires down a few corridors into a gigantic room resembling a huge airplane hangar. In one area, using only ten percent of the total floor space, carpenters had re-created the headquarters of Manchurian Global's President and CEO.

Brought into the CEO's office, I found myself with several of the film's stars. The room became still while the Assistant Director placed people in position. Everything seemed so exacting, precisely measured. It took me a few minutes to realize the Assistant Director who was placing the actors in positions, was taking direction from Jonathan Demme via his headset. Demme watched a monitor in another room and could see what the film would look like on screen. After we were in place, Demme came onto the set and gave each extra something to do during the scene. He told me to watch the large TV screen on the wall because the President was giving a speech during which he was to be assassinated. He told me to take out my cell phone when I saw the assassination and yell (silently) into the phone to let someone know our plan had failed. The wrong man had been shot.

I'm on screen in the *Manchurian Candidate* for 4.5 seconds. But, for me, it was 4.5 on the Richter scale. Watching the principal actors rehearse and do their work convinced me to take the next step. I mailed over 100 headshots and acting resumes to casting directors throughout New York City and, to my wonderful surprise, several called me in to audition.

CHAPTER 31

A school district secretary called me at home the day after the *Manchurian Candidate* shoot. She requested attendance information.

"While you've been on home-assignment, have you had any sick days, vacation days, or other non-work days? If so, you need to document this and let me know on a weekly basis if you are not at your work location which is your home."

"Why are you telling me this now? Are you confirming that the guy in the pickup truck is still monitoring me?" They knew I was gone all day.

I hung up feeling a bit crazed. But, at least I knew Guevara and I weren't nuts. Those men really were watching. Only now did I realize they had moved a couple of blocks away so they could see me sneaking to my car. It was easier for me to accept their presence, easier than not knowing. I waved to them as I passed by.

Guevara and I could not figure out if the men who parked by his and my homes were working for the District, for Parkman, or for somebody else. I didn't care who they worked for. I was now focusing on acting rather than Clearwater. Chris Watkins would have to interrupt my "new life" from this point forward if I needed to focus on Clearwater.

More than 30 years after my last professional acting experience, I was considered a new face but I had a solid resume from my earlier stage work. Now, I wanted film work rather than stage. I decided to continue doing background "acting" as I did on *Manchurian Candidate*, to see if I enjoyed the environment. Most actors my age are very experienced and look upon background work with disdain. I thought of it as a classroom. Each time I worked background, it was like going to school. It wasn't real acting but it was better than sitting home thinking about the investigation. Background work allowed me to watch directors, assistant directors, photographers and actors. I saw how they worked. I learned the vocabulary. My acting teachers told me to stay away from background work because I'd get a reputation as a "background actor" rather than an actor. However, I did not want to give up the learning experiences. So, I continued but stopped telling my teachers about the background work.

In my first meeting with Naomi Kolstein, a woman who would become my agent, she gave me the best advice about background work: "Do the background work if you really think you're learning something. Just stay away from the camera. Don't let them put your face on camera. Just use it as a classroom."

I did that kind of anonymous background work on such TV shows as *Third Watch, Law and Order,* and *Ed.* I am also in deep background on several films including *Lord of War, Game Six,* and *Then She Found Me.* Although I tried to hide in the scenes, my size and new face, sometimes caused directors to select me from among the background actors to do something special. That's when my lack of experience resulted in serious errors that I was glad to make in background rather than a higher level of work.

At a *Third Watch* television shoot, standing among a group of seven or eight men costumed as Hasidic Jews, I stood six inches above the others. Suddenly, the director yelled, "Hey, big guy, I have something special for you to do."

All the other Hasids looked at me. I shrugged my shoulders in the Hasidic manner and went to the director. It was only my second experience since *Manchurian Candidate.* I was not prepared for my first embarrassing mistake outside the comfort of an acting class.

"When the traffic light turns green," the director said, "I want you to take this little kid's hand and run across the street, looking over your shoulder as if you were trying to avoid the police. Then cross the other street and run into that jewelry store with the kid."

It seemed pretty clear to me. I took the kid's hand, waited for the light to turn green, pulled on him and ran halfway across the street before I heard the director yelling for all to hear, "What the hell are you doing?"

I stood dumbfounded in the middle of New York's Grand Street and tried to think of an answer.

"You said to run across the street when the light turned green."

"Whatever happened to lights, camera, rolling, sound, action?"

I looked at him and told him the truth, "I was so excited about being given something special to do on only my third job that I forgot about everything else."

Instead of throwing me back into the crowd and taking somebody with more experience, he acknowledged my honesty and we moved on.

I started attending actor seminars run by casting directors, producers, and agents. They conduct seminars on audition technique and other aspects of an acting career. Over a four month period, I attended more than ten different seminars, each of which was limited to fewer than 20 actors. Again, I found myself in groups where the average age was younger than my own children.

In these seminars, the leaders speak for 20 minutes before responding to questions. Then, the actors leave the room and are called in to audition privately for the presenter. I received feedback about my acting, audition technique, voice, and anything that might improve my auditions.

While getting audition practice at the seminars, I decided to do a real audition for a student film. Other actors told me working in student films would be a good learning experience if the student director was in a graduate program at NYU, Columbia, or New York Film Academy. Very quickly, I landed four leading roles in student films that gave me on-camera experience and enough footage to assemble a three-minute reel that represented my acting skills, a video resume.

I mailed the reel to 30 casting directors in New York City, one of whom, Sig DeMiguel, called me for an audition. He asked if I owned a Hasidic hat. I didn't own one but said I did. He asked me to bring it to audition the next day.

After racing to hat shops and Halloween costume shops, I finally found something similar to a Hasidic hat and arrived at Sig's office, hat in hand. This was my first audition for a speaking role in a big league film. The film was, *Brooklyn Rules*, starring Alec Baldwin, Freddie Prinze Jr., Jerry Ferrara and Scott Caan. Sitting in the waiting room, I suddenly had great misgivings, feeling like I was auditioning at a level for which I was not ready. I'd only done speaking roles in student films but Sig was very positive, "This part is yours... I know you can do this...they're gonna love you..."

He asked me to quickly learn a few lines from the script and say them on-camera. He videotaped my audition and sent it off to the director. The next day he called to tell me I had booked the job. It was a SAG film; meaning only union members could act in this film. So, I had to join the Screen Actors Guild, something for which actors pray. An actor cannot join SAG unless he has a job that requires union membership, and I'd done that after only a few months, instead of the many years it usually takes.

I arrived at the shoot an hour before my call time because I was so excited. The set was a jewelry store on Chambers Street in lower Manhattan. I knew from the script that Jerry Ferrara ("Turtle" on *Entourage*), Freddy Prinze Jr., and I were the only characters in the scene. So, I was shocked when I turned the corner onto Chambers Street and saw literally dozens of technicians, lighting specialists, and others as well as a full city block of trailers.

I found the production coordinator and asked where I should start my day. She was surprised to see me that early.

"Why don't you go hang out in your trailer for an hour or so and I'll call you when we're ready to bring you to makeup and wardrobe."

"My trailer?" She saw the stunned look on my face.

"The third set of trailers has three doors. Freddie, Jerry and you." It was hard not to smile.

When I got to my trailer, I learned why they had called three days earlier to ask what I like as hot and cold beverages. My trailer room was well stocked with both. I called friends and relatives to tell them how excited I was to be calling them from my own trailer on a movie shoot.

CHAPTER 32

In the midst of this personal euphoria created by my involvement in this film, Chris Watkins called to warn that I'd soon receive official charges and a hearing summons. The hearing was to determine my competency to serve as an administrator.

We were given a list of State Education Department Arbitration Judges, and asked to select three. The District did the same. There was concurrence on one arbitrator. He was assigned by the State Education Department to conduct a hearing on my competence.

We did not know that this arbitrator had served on a corporate board with one of the District's lawyers and was friends with another of their lawyers. The arbitrator announced this during the third day of testimony. We had wondered why he continuously referred to the District's lawyers by first name and to my attorney as "Mr. Watkins." Now we knew.

The hearing took six days of testimony over a year's time due to the schedules of all involved. Months passed between each day of testimony. The passage of time gave some witnesses an excuse to have memory issues. It shocked me when witnesses had such bad memory loss that they denied any knowledge of the Parkman-Seth relationship. Some of the deniers were witnesses with whom I had personally shared my concerns. I knew they knew about the relationship. "Incompetency" charges were not filed against any other mandated reporters who admitted awareness of the relationship but failed to file the same "report" being used to determine my competency.

At this and other hearings, my supervisors finally admitted I had reported concerns to them. They ignored my reports, according to their testimonies, because they thought I was lying. They felt I "was after the Superintendent's job," just what Parkman wanted them to believe. Understandably, they believed him because my concerns seemed impossible. It would have been easier to convince people the sky was falling than to convince them Bob Parkman was molesting a child. He seemed as pious as a Catholic priest, and as righteous as a Scout Master. Until Seth, Parkman seemed ready for sainthood, and although they saw Parkman's obsession and its public relations impact, my supervisors could not accept the possibility of molestation.

When Chris Watkins showed the arbitrator that other staff knew even more than I about the relationship but failed to report Parkman, the arbitrator responded, "they are not on trial here, Mr. Cohen is." Not only did the arbitrator ignore such evidence, he turned an "administrative hearing" into a "trial." It wasn't difficult to predict his conclusions.

Three police department representatives testified that I reported my concerns to them and had many follow-up discussions detailing Parkman's visits to the school. Police also testified they filed no incident reports until Parkman's arrest and directed me to file no written reports because they would interfere with their investigation.

After hearing police testify that I was the only educator who reported Parkman, the arbitrator still decided I should be terminated for failing to "correctly" report Parkman on a written form, and for changing test scores. He refused to consider that I was the only person who actually reported concerns to the police. He refused to consider that police told me not to prepare any written reports. And, he refused to consider that I reported to my supervisors, none of whom, except the Board President, attempted to stop Parkman. I immediately felt he would be overturned in the courts.

The Arbitrator did not consider that I signed each changed test in one of the two required places, and was not hiding the changes. Every year, auditors from the State select a sampling of tests from every high school for re-scoring by the State. If such an error had been found by their review, the State would have written a memo about the error and suggested re-training on test scoring procedures. In this instance, the School Board found the error rather than the State and used it to end my career.

After the Arbitrator's suggestion to fire me, I suspected the School Board would vote to terminate me at the next Board meeting. I raced up to the State capitol and officially retired two days before the board meeting. The next day, I informed the District's Personnel Director I had retired. The School Board voted to terminate me even though I was officially retired. This eliminated my retirement health benefits. Chris Watkins immediately filed suit for wrongful termination and violation of my first amendment right to speak out without retaliation. My lawsuit was based on the fact that I had spoken very publicly about my reporting to District officials about Parkman, after which I was fired by those to whom I reported.

During the months it took to hear from the Federal Court regarding my lawsuit, I focused on acting. Kolstein signed me to an agent contract and strongly urged me to audition for stage as well as film.

"You have a big face, visible from 30 rows back. Stage directors will love your face. You have a great voice, it booms. They'll love that too. And, you can act."

I successfully auditioned for two shows in New York City. These shows gave me Manhattan stage experience and positive reviews.

Suddenly, I was a busy actor. I got to act at the famous La Mama Theatre and other historic venues. I was attending rehearsals, working with professional actors, and meeting directors and writers. I also joined a weekly actor's study group. We rented rehearsal space and brought seven actors together to practice things we could not do in class, things like having a heart attack or feeling extreme pain.

Networking began to click for me. Acting jobs came from people with whom I had worked on earlier shoots or stage productions. A sound technician on one of the earlier student films was now directing a feature film. He called me for a role in *Minority*. An Assistant Director on a low-budget film, *My Mother's Fairy Tales*, called me to a bigger-budget film starring Eli Wallach and Annie Parisse. And so it went. One job begat another. I was a new face on the block and had a positive attitude. I was thankful for any role, no matter how small. I took that attitude wherever I went and it seemed to get me more acting work.

During that time I also got into Actor's Equity and AFTRA, the stage actor's union and the TV Union. This immediately doubled the number of auditions for which I was eligible. Every job was a classroom for me, especially when I acted with such talents as Lena Olin, Jesse Eisenberg, Katherine Heigl, Sean Penn, and others from whom I took on-the-job training. I also got my first lead in an indie film and considered myself a full-time working actor. As of this writing, I've been in six New York shows, including a one-man show, *ABBIE*, in which I played Abbie Hoffman. Since that show closed in 2011, I've focused on film acting and had major roles opposite several Hollywood stars.

Five years after Parkman was jailed, he was released. Ironically during the same month, the New York State Education Department cancelled my teaching and administration licenses in support of my termination.

Parkman was free but my own professional punishment would now begin. Although the State gave me an opportunity to explain my case, they supported their arbitrator's recommendation and ignored our claims that the Arbitrator facilitated a wrongful firing and violated my first amendment rights to speak without fear of retaliation. After we sued the District in Federal Court for violating my rights, the District agreed to pay me $425,000 rather than fight in court. The State ignored their payment in removing my licenses.

The acting profession has become my life and the field of education has sadly left me. I was a committed teacher and supervisor, and I still believe education is the key to our world's eventual success.

Personal vindication came in the form of the District's cash settlement. But, it is important that stories of sexual perversity in our schools be told. Parents and teachers need to be more vigilant and will only be so when more stories are shared.

School district doors are now closed to me because they took my licenses. The knowledge that Seth is saved, that Parkman was found guilty, and that my roles in both are clear to all, makes those shut school doors invisible to me. I see the hypocrisy behind the doors, the pedophilia that hypocrisy protects, and hope that Parkman's story of the devout, committed educator shakes loose the many other stories that need to be told.

POSTSCRIPT

After I wrote and was sharing this book, people asked, "what happened to Seth, to Parkman, to you, to others?"

Parkman - The former Superintendent was sentenced to five years in State Prison after avoiding a public trial by copping a plea. Upon sentencing, he was transferred from County Jail to a State Transition Facility in Fishkill, New York. In Fishkill, Parkman was placed in a holding cell with 15 other prisoners awaiting intake and transfer to their various long-term facilities.

For some reason, the guards left the area for a minute, at which time Parkman was severely beaten and almost killed by the inmates who knew he was a child-molester. According to newspaper reports, Parkman required surgery to save his vision after one of his eye sockets was busted by a kick to the head. He was then transferred to a more isolated setting in upstate New York.

Guards in that remote prison told guards at Williamsport Prison, near Clearwater, about Parkman's daily activities. Williamsport guards shared the information with guys on my security team who were former Williamsport guards. That is how we knew Parkman was in a cell corridor with several other child-molesters and spent much of his first few months reading the Bible.

Apparently he was not a model prisoner, staying by himself after having arguments in common areas with several prisoners who saw newspaper articles about him. He became a sullen isolate.

Chris Watkins and I interviewed Parkman in prison after he was there about a year, asking questions to assist my legal case. Parkman was recalcitrant with seemingly no remorse about having destroyed my career and the careers of others. "If people thought I was doing something wrong, why didn't they stop me," he said. Chris responded, "I think they did and that's why you're here." He denied having organized a multifaceted plan to get rid of me, one that his staff continued after his arrest. He said the boy lied about that and many other things.

Parkman eventually requested parole and even convinced one of his former Cabinet members to be his parole sponsor with the condition he could not use the Cabinet member's home address as his potential parolee residence. Freedom of Information showed that Parkman, still believing in his infallibility, gave the parole board the address of an abandoned factory in Clearwater. Did he think they wouldn't check?

No parole applications were accepted from Parkman after that bogus attempt and he served his full five-year sentence. Parkman has been released and is now a registered sex offender. His address is published on sex offender websites. At this time, he is unemployed, living on his pension and Social Security as an isolate in a distant part of the country where the real estate is cheap, nobody asks questions and it's easier to live out life as a registered sex offender, former School Superintendent.

Seth - Now employed at a major retailer near Clearwater after graduating near the top of his class at Bedford High. According to Dr. Guevara, who was shopping and happened to meet Seth at his job, the young man seems happy and well-adjusted to his situation. He also attends college on a part-time basis and plans to attend full-time.

Seth's family sued the Clearwater School District and was granted a pre-trial settlement of $950,000. After giving pre-trial depositions, the District's insurance company decided to avoid the public trial, as they did with me.

Bernard H. Cohen – I became Bern Cohen the actor instead of Bernard H. Cohen the education administrator. I was lucky enough to get cast in six New York stage shows, including three musicals. During the past eight years, I've had roles in over 30 movies, including several leads in films with Hollywood stars.

While writing this book, I filmed such movies as *This Must Be The Place* (Sean Penn), *Holy Rollers* (Jesse Eisenberg), *Devil You Know* (Lena Olin), *Frank vs. God* (Henry Ian Cusick) and *Doctor Bello* (Isaiah Washington). In the last three I had major roles which included all the Hollywood trappings that were great fun.

I'm a full-time actor going to auditions, taking classes, and upgrading the skills of my new trade. The stage and film work, in many ways, helped me close my Clearwater era. I went from the ongoing frustration of saving Seth to the frustrations of the legal system to a new career that kept me very busy when down-time would have been depressing.

It has been a thrill to achieve such quick success as an actor and it has been fun to share the acting experiences with hundreds of my former Clearwater students and their families via social networks. Quite often, parents of my students share uplifting stories about their children being surprised to see me in a movie. One parent recently emailed that her daughter stood up while her University of Arizona dorm was watching "*27 Dresses*," and yelled out proudly, 'That's my High School Principal!'" That email brought tears to my eyes. I had all those kids grabbed away from me, but they are still there for me.

For the latest update on my acting career, check out my page at imdb.com

Dr. Fletcher and other School Board members were denied positions on the Board at the next election. I met with and walked with several candidates running against the then incumbent members. The community was very supportive of me and the candidates I backed. I stood at supermarket entrances and met hundreds of parents at weekend athletic events. When I was suspended, I was not permitted on school property but Clearwater's weekend juvenile soccer attracted thousands and was not a school function or on school grounds. The Board was swept clean of those who supported the pedophile. This election even included a successful run by an 18-year-old recent CHS graduate, Paul Roy, now a New York television reporter.

District Supervisors – None of the senior staff who ignored our expressed concerns or who actually worked against our attempts to save Seth is employed in Clearwater. The top administrators retired or resigned before any complacency issues were discussed by the incoming Board. Current students know nothing of this terrible interruption in the District's evolution, and life goes on. New leaders are leading the District and learning from past mistakes.

High School Staff – There are two groups of High School staff who were hurt by their outspoken support of me; those no longer employed by Clearwater and those still on the District payroll.

The Director of Guidance, the Chairman of Social Studies, the Director of Security, the disciplinary-program coordinator; They all lost their after-school positions and/or extra position salaries because they spoke out at School Board meetings on behalf of me and our fight to save Seth. All these professionals are either retired or working in other districts. I can publicly acknowledge them.

There is another group of outspoken teachers who are still working at CHS or at other schools in Clearwater. They also spoke publicly in support of my efforts and also lost their extra salaried positions as athletic coaches and club advisors. I cannot mention the currently-employed teachers because there are still some politicians in Clearwater who think we were wrong to cause a city-wide upheaval by reporting our boss as a child-molester. The individuals who spoke out on my behalf have lost thousands of dollars in coaching and club stipends after their bravery left them vulnerable.

It took a team to fight. We won but many also lost. I am certain the same will happen at Penn State and other locations where people speak out. But, speak we must until the many stories out there bring an end to such abuse by the pedophiles who are truly the Jekyll-Hydes of our society.

The articles on the following
pages are provided

Times Herald-Record   Friday, January 10, 2003

Page **4**

School superintendent behind bars: *A community is shaken*

Superintendent facing child sex abuse charge

By Jessica Gardner,
Oliver Mackson
and Greg Cannon
Times Herald-Record

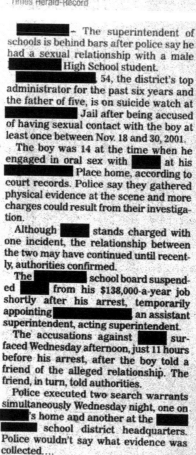

████████ – The superintendent of schools is behind bars after police say he had a sexual relationship with a male ████████ High School student.

████████ 54, the district's top administrator for the past six years and the father of five, is on suicide watch at ████████ Jail after being accused of having sexual contact with the boy at least once between Nov. 18 and 30, 2001.

The boy was 14 at the time when he engaged in oral sex with ████ at his ████████ Place home, according to court records. Police say they gathered physical evidence at the scene and more charges could result from their investigation.

Although ████ stands charged with one incident, the relationship between the two may have continued until recently, authorities confirmed.

The ████████ school board suspended ████ from his $138,000-a-year job shortly after his arrest, temporarily appointing ████████ an assistant superintendent, acting superintendent.

The accusations against ████ surfaced Wednesday afternoon, just 11 hours before his arrest, after the boy told a friend of the alleged relationship. The friend, in turn, told authorities.

Police executed two search warrants simultaneously Wednesday night, one on ████'s home and another at the ████ school district headquarters. Police wouldn't say what evidence was collected....

Times Herald-Record Tuesday, January 14, 2003

Times Herald-Record/MICHELE HASKELL

███████ center, suspended superintendent of ███████ schools, appears in ███████ Court yesterday for a preliminary hearing on charges he sexually abused a 14-year-old boy ███████ appeared in court without a lawyer.

Officials silent on ███████ issue

Meanwhile, accused superintendent stands before judge

By Jessica Gardner
and Greg Cannon
Times Herald-Record

███████ School officials offered their annual state of the district message yesterday, billed as a gathering to inform the public of issues "in light of our most troubling events."

Those events stemming from the arrest of the man who had led the district for seven years, never came up. That silence drowned out the rest of the message.

Officials never mentioned his name, or what they planned to do now that Superintendent ███████ ███████ stands charged with sodomizing a 15-year-old male student. They didn't say what they would do to make sure it doesn't happen again.

Just one week ago, he was their leader. Now, he was dead to them. He had disappeared.

Across town the ███████ City courtroom door swung open and ███████ was led in by two armed police officers. His head was down, his hands bound in front of his body with heavy silver handcuffs.

It was ███████ preliminary hearing, his first court appearance since being locked away in lieu of $500,000 bail Thursday

morning.

His gray hair was neatly combed and he was dressed in the same maroon pullover and faded jeans he was wearing the day he was arrested.

The 34-year-old father of five stood alone in the courtroom. He acted oblivious to the two television cameras set up in the nearby jury box or the photographer snapping his picture.

He kept his eyes focused on City Court Judge ███████ ███████ answering each question posed to him with a polite "Yes, Sir."

When asked if he had retained an attorney, ███████ evenly replied, "My wife and I are in the process of doing so."

'These are very dark times. Our difficulties are not behind us and there are undoubtedly troubles before us.'

███████ ███████
school board president

asked if ███████ had anyone in particular in mind, ███████ asked, "May I just say 'Yes,'" ███████ made no objection.

The hearing, a procedural requirement under state law, was postponed until this after-noon pending the convening of an ███████ County grand jury.

The grand jury is expected to hear evidence today against ███████ on charges that he had a sexual relationship with a high school student in the district.

The student and ███████ City detectives who investigated the case are expected to testify.

The grand jury can choose to do one of three things. It can dismiss charges of felony

sodomy and misdemeanor endangering the welfare of a child against ███████ indict him on the existing charges or choose to add additional charges to the indictment.

A decision is expected by the end of the week, at the latest. If for some reason the grand jury does not meet today, ███████ explained that ███████ would be released without bail pending further court action, in accordance with the law.

Cops say they've got a strong case against ███████ including witness accounts, physical evidence and an interview ███████ participated in Wednesday night. Since his arrest, no other alleged victims have come forward to claim abuse at the hands of the superintendent.

Meanwhile, just minutes after ███████ shuffled out of the courtroom to return to his cell in the ███████ County Jail, his colleagues were gathering in the school district offices.

"These are very dark times," said board President ███████ ███████. "Our difficulties are not behind us and there are undoubtedly troubles before us."

Not once during their brief, prepared remarks did school officials refer to the suspended superintendent, directly or indirectly.

Acting Superintendent ███████

Police seek information

Authorities stressed that anyone with information related to the case should contact them at ███████ ███████

Do you have questions?

Do you need help talking to your children about what happened? Call or e-mail us. Questions will be forwarded to ███████ ███████ psychologist ███████ and a selection of answers will be published at a later date.
On the Web:
www.recordonline.com
Call-in hot line: ███████

███████ said the district's desire to keep the public informed was limited by legal considerations. "It's an issue and it has to be talked about," ███████ said of the arrest, but added, "to the best of our ability."

Instead officials spoke of aching hearts, commitment to students, and rebuilding integrity as they sought to reassure everyone that the district is putting the matter behind it.

But they never spoke his name.

Reporter Maureen Nandini Mitra contributed to this story.

Times Herald-Record Wednesday, January 15, 2003

'The whole building knew'

Board talked to ███ about boy, source says

By Greg Cannon, Jessica Gardner, Steve Israel
and Maureen Nandini Mitra
Times Herald-Record

███ – The ███ school board knew of a relationship between suspended Superintendent ███ ███ and the 15-year-old male high school student he's accused of molesting before ███'s arrest last week, a source close to the board said yesterday.

Board members talked to ███ about the boy several months ago in a closed-door meeting called specifically to address concerns about the relationship, said the source, who asked not to be identified.

"Something was brought up in executive session that he ███ may have pulled the kid out of class a lot," the source said. "But there was nothing that would raise a question of impropriety of a sexual relationship.

"The whole building knew ███ was mentoring the kid," the source said.

Since ███'s arrest Thursday, questions have spread throughout the district about the arrest and what the board might have known about events leading up to it.

"There's a real buzz out there," ███ Mayor ███ said. "Parents are concerned about the whole system."

███ High School health teacher ███, a frequent critic of the administration and former football coach who was once suspended by ███ said the existence of some type of relationship, if not the specifics of it, was common knowledge in the district.

"Apart from the sexual stuff, the school board knew about the kid for a year," ███ said. "It's been the topic of conversation around the school for at least a year.

"He ███ has taken the kid out of [class] 30 or 40 times this year in the high school alone.

"The school board knew what was going on, and they have to answer some questions," ███ said. "Like how did they allow this obsessive relationship? They established an atmosphere for that superintendent to let him get away with it."

Meanwhile, school district officials, already operating under their own veil of secrecy, issued a gag order yesterday to all district administrators, ordering them to keep quiet about the suspended superintendent.

Specifically, the memo from Acting Superintendent ███ directs them to give a scripted response to press inquiries about what, if anything, they knew about a relationship between ███ and the student.

Contacted yesterday, school board members and administrators mostly stuck to that script. . . .

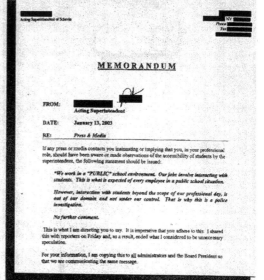

Acting Superintendent of Schools

███ NY ███
Phone
Fax

MEMORANDUM

FROM: ███
Acting Superintendent

DATE: January 13, 2003

RE: Press & Media

If any press or media contacts you insinuating or implying that you, in your professional role, should have been aware or made observations of the accessibility of students by the superintendent, the following statement should be issued:

"We work in a "PUBLIC" school environment. Our jobs involve interacting with students. This is what is expected of every employee in a public school situation.

However, interaction with students beyond the scope of our professional day, is out of our domain and not under our control. That is why this is a police investigation.

No further comment.

This is what I am directing you to say. It is imperative that you adhere to this. I shared this with reporters on Friday and, as a result, ended what I considered to be unnecessary speculation.

For your information, I am copying this to all administrators and the Board President so that we are communicating the same message.

224

Times Herald-Record Friday, January 17, 2003

Complaints made against ▆▆▆▆▆▆ months ago

By Greg Cannon and Jessica Gardner
Times Herald-Record

▆▆▆▆▆▆ – The ▆▆▆▆▆▆ school board acknowledged last night that it received complaints months ago about the conduct of suspended Superintendent ▆▆▆▆▆▆ ▆▆▆▆▆ with regard to a student in the school district.

Complaints about ▆▆▆▆'s "educational interference" involving a student were brought to the board's attention in the spring of 2002 and the board "demanded that interference to cease immediately," board President ▆▆▆▆▆▆ said.

▆▆▆▆ did not elaborate on what the "educational interference" involved or identify the student in question, citing confidentiality laws.

But sources close to the district confirmed that ▆▆▆▆ had repeatedly signed out of school the 15-year-old male student he is accused of molesting, and interfered with disciplinary actions against the boy.

▆▆▆▆▆▆ drew a clear distinction between the actions that prompted complaints to the board and the ones that lead to ▆▆▆▆'s arrest last week. Only after that arrest did the board learn of allegations against ▆▆▆▆ of "misconduct of a sexual nature," ▆▆▆ said.

"The board never had information of molestation or sexual abuse prior to last week," ▆▆▆▆▆▆ said. Had any such allegations come to the board's attention, they would have been reported to authorities, ▆▆▆ said.

▆▆▆▆▆▆ remarks came during what she called a "forum" held during a break in a closed-door board meeting "to end speculation that the board stood by passively or engaged in a cover-up." ▆▆▆▆▆▆ took no questions during or after the forum.

▆▆▆ said that police have not informed the board of the alleged victim's identity, and it's not the board's place to speculate about it.

▆▆▆ said the board is cooperating with police. Police said Wednesday that they are planning to question board members as to who knew what when.

Still unanswered is the question of whether ▆▆▆▆ will continue to draw his $138,000 yearly salary while suspended. The board's attorney is reviewing ▆▆▆▆'s contract before making a recommendation to the board.

The room at the district's ▆▆▆▆ Avenue administration building was packed with principals, teachers and staff. ▆▆▆▆▆▆ High School principal Bernard Cohen was among them. He refused to answer questions about the board's comments, but said, "I can tell you our school is pulled together. Everybody is focused on education."

Staff writer John-Henry Doucette contributed to this story.

225

Times Herald-Record Saturday, January 25, 2003

Board disciplined ███████, then gave him contract, raise

**By John-Henry Doucette
and Greg Cannon**
Times Herald-Record

████████ – The ████████ school board last year gave Superintendent ████████ a contract extension and a raise just a few months after disciplining him for "educational interference" with a boy he is now accused of sexually abusing, records show.

The board last spring ordered ████ to stop interfering with a then-14-year-old ████████ High School student.

It is not unusual for an administrator to renegotiate a contract long before it is set to expire. But in this case, it came a few months after the closed-door rebuke of ████ which was made public this month.

Last night, school board Vice President ████████ referred questions to board President ████████. But ████ suggested ████'s actions, as the board understood them, were not necessarily cause for alarm.

"Some people understood it to be a kid being pulled out of class once or twice and a mentor who took a kid under his wing and maybe was a little too exuberant about it," ████ said.

City police arrested ████ Jan. 8 and charged him with sodomy, child endangerment and several counts of sexual abuse.

He remains in ████ County Jail.

████ and ████ signed a new contract on Sept. 12, 2002.

The district released the contract yesterday at the request of the Times Herald-Record.

The deal increased ████'s annual salary from $133,327 to $143,327 and extended his contract, which was to expire in 2005, by another year.

████████ would not say why the board gave a raise and a longer term to an employee it had recently rebuked.

"I'm not free to comment on that," ████ said. "I believe that's all I'm going to say about the entire case. I will let it be played out in court where the truth will be revealed."

Tuesday, April 1, 2003

Our Towns

TIMES HERALD-RECORD • WWW.RECORDONLINE.COM

New target: high school principal

By John-Henry Doucette
Times Herald-Record

█████ – School administrators, already embroiled in the ███ sex scandal, have launched an internal investigation into accusations against ██████ High School principal Bernard Cohen.

"Retaliation," Cohen called it.

Cohen, 60, was credited with cleaning up problem schools in the New York City system until now Acting Superintendent ████ ████████ recruited him to come to ██ ████████ back when ██ was an assistant superintendent.

Now the district is investigating Cohen on anonymous accusations that he took petty cash, changed grades and ran a hostile workplace, according to sources who attended an early morning staff meeting during which ████████ made the allegations known. . . .

He said the accusations – and ████████ public announcement of them in front of more than 100 high school employees – are an attempt to intimidate district employees and retaliate for his testimony before an ████████ County grand jury investigating the scandal. . . .

Nonsense, said Cohen and his lawyers, ████████ and Christopher Watkins of the Chester firm Thornton, Bergstein & Ullrich. They said the district has played hardball with Cohen since he refused to meet with their last "investigator." . . .

"They needed Bernie to participate in the cover-up," ██████ said. "But he's not going to join in their circling of the wagons.".

Cohen said he tried to alert ████████ and then-school board President ████████ about ████s troubling behavior more than a year before city cops arrested ████ Due to such concerns, the board last year disciplined ████ for "educational interference" with the student. . . .

Wednesday, April 2, 2003

Our Towns

TIMES HERALD-RECORD • WWW.RECORDONLINE.COM

Principal: Delays did damage

District's inaction led to further alleged abuse, Cohen says

By John-Henry Doucette
Times Herald-Record
jdoucette@th-record.com

███████ – When Bernard Cohen told ██████ his suspicions about ███████'s relationship with a young boy, he said he was told, "What can we do? He's the superintendent."

Cohen, the ███████ High School principal, said that conversation took place in November 2001. It was several months before the school board disciplined ██████ for "educational interference" with a student – his alleged victim.

██████ is now jailed on charges he sexually abused the boy.

According to Cohen, suspicions of an improper relationship – and rumors of sex – between a boy and the district's top official were more widespread than previously disclosed to the public by school officials.

Had the district acted sooner, Cohen said, some of the damage from the scandal could have been mitigated.

Despite repeated efforts by Cohen and others at the high school to get the boy – and report ██████ to police – top ██████ schools officials delayed action, Cohen said.

██████ the district's acting superintendent, yesterday refused to address specific comments made by Cohen. She asserted she never suspected sex between ██████ and the boy.

"We had a superintendent in our midst that was ill and we didn't realize it," ██████ said.

But, according to Cohen, delays by district leaders led to:
- Continued alleged abuse and a clearly unusual relationship. In fact, Cohen said it took a threat by 10 high school employees to "out" ██████ during a televised school board meeting in the spring of 2002 to pressure the board to discipline ██████. They did so privately that April. Cohen said he first raised concerns with then-board President ██████ in January, three months earlier.
- A cover-up since ██████'s Jan. 2 arrest that includes intimidation and bogus accusations against those who testified before an ██████ County grand jury investigating the district's actions in the scandal.
- Pressure by ██████ to keep his accuser at ██████ High School when educators felt it was in the boy's best interest to go to a special education facility.

Cohen spoke Monday during a wide-ranging interview with the Times Herald-Record. It took place hours after the district announced an investigation of anonymous complaints that Cohen misused petty cash, changed grades and ran a hostile work environment.

Cohen described these allegations as retaliation against him by district officials.

Cohen said his suspicions were aroused 18 months before ██████'s arrest in January.

In the spring of 2001, ██████ told Cohen about an articulate kid who, Cohen would learn, spent afternoons at ██████'s office, caught rides with him and publicly called the district's top administrator " ██████ " Cohen said.

The boy was coming to the high school in the fall of 2001. ██████

Bernard Cohen, principal of ██████ High School, speaks during an interview Monday at the office of his lawyers, Watkins of Thornton, Bergstein & Ullrich in Chester. Cohen said suspicions of an improper relationship – and rumors of sex – between a boy and the district's top official were more widespread than previously thought.

Times Herald-Record/TOM BUSHEY

> ### 'We had a superintendent in our midst that was ill and we didn't realize it.'
> ██████, acting School District superintendent

"We're conducting an investigation into the merit of allegations made against Mr. Cohen," ██████ said. "It has nothing to do with the ██████ case."

"taking care" of his discipline.

Cohen, as school principal, is a so-called mandated reporter – someone required by law to report suspected child abuse. "I called the police," Cohen said.

Police Lt. ██████ said yesterday that the first conversation between Cohen and Sgt. ██████ happened in June 2001. At least twice, the boy denied a sexual relationship with ██████ while talking to police. It took until Jan. 4, 2003, for the boy to contact city police. ██████ picked up that night.

Cohen said he and others repeatedly tried to force the dis-

██████ Middle School staffers warned some at the high school what was headed their way, and they reported it to Cohen.

Cohen heard tales about ██████ pulling the boy out of class and ██████

trict to deal with the problem. It did not, he said.

In early 2002, Cohen said he spoke to ██████ about it and, once, handed him a six-page memorandum detailing his concerns and some comments made by ██████ about the boy.

He sat there and watched by ██████ read it, he said.

Cohen said, "He told me he and [current board President] ██████ already had a lengthy conversation with ██████ about the manner in which his relationship with the boy was being perceived." ██████ told me he would take immediate action ... Weeks went by. We saw no change."

Cohen said he went back to ██████ who told him, "Bern, you don't even see the half of it."

Cohen said ██████ complained that the boy was always in administrative offices after school.

Once, ██████ said the boy had called ██████ " an informality" that Cohen said ██████ resented. Cohen said ██████ told him about a party for ██████ where one administrator joked about ██████ kissing the boy.

Weeks went by again, Cohen

said, and some at the high school decided to take matters into their own hands.

"A group of teachers said they were going to go to a meeting and point a finger," Cohen said.

██████ caught wind of this, and Cohen said he came to the high school to talk to Cohen and ██████ a school psychologist who has also criticized the district's handling of ██████.

Cohen was told by ██████ that he had taken care of it, and that ██████ would be disciplined and could lose his job if he did not stop seeing the boy.

██████ did not return a call yesterday in his office.

"██████ came to me and said he had, to stop seeing the boy," Cohen said. "He said how sad he was to give up a relationship with a young boy he felt really needed him. I told him perception is reality, and the perception was he was [engaged in a sexual relationship with him]."

A few months later, the school board voted ██████ a contract extension and a raise.

Now the district faces a $61 million damages claim by the boy's family.

Tuesday, April 15, 2003

Our Towns

TIMES HERALD-RECORD • WWW.RECORDONLINE.COM

School board warned ███ of bond with boy

By John-Henry Doucette
and Jessica Gardner
Times Herald-Record

███ – The school board may not have suspected its top administrator of having sex with a student last year, but then-President ███ knew ███'s relationship with the boy was fueling speculation.

On April 30, 2002, ███ ordered ███ to cut off contact with the boy in a letter that detailed "a pattern of conduct" by ███.

"This conduct includes interacting with him privately, breakfast and lunch meetings, transporting him in your vehicle, purchasing personal items, and from time to time removing him from school," ███ wrote.

"Most recently, you have intervened in varied disciplinary actions consequent to his actions at the high school," he wrote.

Despite the unusual concerns raised by the relationship, board members said they did not suspect criminal behavior, and they did not call authorities. A few months after issuing the letter to ███ and the rest of the board voted to extend ███'s contract. The deal was signed on Sept. 12, 2002.

Last week, the district released two letters after the Times Herald-Record made a Freedom of Information Law request.

In an interview last week, ███ and current school board President ███ maintained they had not heard of any sexual accusations against ███ at the time the letters were written.

███ was charged Jan. 8 with sodomy, sexual abuse and endangering the welfare of a child.

In the wake of the scandal – a probe by Orange County prosecutors and accusations of a cover-up – the ███ letter of warning seems like prophecy.

"If you continue in this relationship," he wrote, "and the public becomes more aware ... it could cause irreparable damage to you personally, to your family and to the institution that you serve so conscientiously."

He added, "I am directing that you take immediate steps to cease and desist from any further contact with this student, in any form whatsoever."

That did not happen.

In fact, a law enforcement source said ███ had several contacts with the child after the ███ letter was written. For example, the two were seen together outside school.

███ kept the boy's birthday on his work calendar posted at the district Web site.

Billing records show ███ took hundreds of calls from a cell phone the boy often used.

The boy used that phone to call ███ four times in the hours before the arrest, according to the source and records.

"Until [the arrest], everyone on the board understood that ███ was abiding by the letter of counsel," ███ said.

The board members wrote the letters because they said they had no evidence of a sexual relationship.

"It was written in terms of letting him know the potential of what people might say," ███, a school lawyer, said about the ███ letter.

"That was what we talked to him about," ███ said.

"It [was] our way of giving Mr. ███ the full gamut of potential that this relationship would have," ███ added. "Not that we knew of anything."

The other letter was a reminder written Oct. 7 by ███ after ███ told her the boy had called him on the phone.

Though the ███ letter threatened discipline for any contact, ███ wrote. "Be assured that both the spirit and the letter of this communication is not meant to be punitive."

███ said ███ told her of the boy's call so he could remain "above board."

The two letters were kept in ███'s office, although copies were made for ███'s personnel file.

"We didn't want the letters to disappear," ███ explained yesterday. "The superintendent has a key to everything."

███ is suspended as superintendent. He remains in jail. The board has begun a proceeding to fire him.

On the Web:
Visit recordonline.com to view the letters regarding ███ conduct.

Times Herald-Record   Monday, September 22, 2003

███ sentencing today for sodomizing boy, 14

By ███████ Gardner
Times Herald-Record

███ - The former ███████ school superintendent, now a convicted felon and a future registered sex offender, will face judgment today for sodomizing a teenage boy.

███████ whose recent felony conviction will block him from ever working in the education field again, will still receive a state pension.

███ pleaded guilty on July 23 to second-degree sodomy, a felony. He faces a maximum sentence of 1½ to 5½ years in state prison for sexually abusing a student, then age 14. The minimum sentence could be as little as probation.

Despite his conviction, ███ pension will remain intact, said ███████, a spokesman for the New York State Department of Education. The pension will likely exceed $21,000 annually, as estimated by the New York State Teachers' Retirement System online calculator. The estimate is based on his years of service in New York state.

███ has been in ███ County Jail since his Jan. 8 arrest. It's possible he could be sentenced to time he's already served, said ███████ ███ lawyer. "We don't expect his point of release to be now," ███ said, adding his client will likely make some sort of statement at the sentencing.

As part of ███ plea agreement, he will be required to register as a sex offender and give up his teaching certificate in New York state.

███ had not turned in his teaching certificate as of Friday, ███ said. The state Department of Education's Professional Practices and Standards board met Thursday to begin the removal process.

"We're not going to wait on him for that," ███ said.

"There is no opportunity for ███ to work as an educator in a school system ever again," ███ said.

Once action is taken regarding ███ license, the Educator Identity Clearinghouse will be alerted. The clearinghouse, an element of the National Association of State Directors of Teacher Education, provides information to licensing authorities throughout the country about individuals who have surrendered or lost their teaching credentials based on criminal or other inappropriate actions...

Earlier this year, an ███ County grand jury heard weeks of testimony from school district employees to find out what they knew of the relationship between ███ and the 15-year-old male student he admitted to accosting...

The grand jury has been working for months on a report based on thousands of transcribed pages of testimony. The 23-member panel is expected to vote on a final draft in the next couple of weeks, ███ said.

From there, the report will be submitted to the court. It becomes public only after a judge deems that the report's content is supported by sufficient evidence, ███ said.

Times Herald-Record   Tuesday, October 21, 2003

District's probe of principal shifts to ███ issue

By Nathan Hegedus
Times Herald-Record

██████ – The investigation was supposed to be about petty cash and changing grades.

Suddenly it is about ████████, the former school superintendent convicted of sodomizing a male student.

A ████████ School District investigation into ████████ High School Principal Bernard Cohen has shifted from questions of his day-to-day activities to what staff members knew about ███ and the boy, according to Cohen's lawyer.

"It is a ham-handed way to get information they're not entitled to," said Christopher Watkins, a lawyer with Thornton, Bergstein & Ullrich. "If the taxpayers knew how much money is being spent [on the investigation], they would be up in arms about it."

The district opened its investigation of Cohen in April after it received anonymous accusations that he took money, changed grades and ran a hostile workplace.

At the time, school board President ████████ said the investigation was not related to the ███ case.

Yesterday, ████████ said she could not comment on the direction of the investigation before it is completed.

"The only purpose of the investigation is to safeguard the well-being of our students and the integrity of the educational process," she said. "That is the only reason that we continue."

Cohen has called the investigation baseless "retaliation" for his criticism of the district's handling of the ███ affair. Cohen said he tried to alert Acting Superintendent ████████ and former board President ████████ about ███'s behavior more than a year before the arrest.

The board subsequently disciplined ███ for "educational interference" with the student, but ███ continued his relationship with the teen.

After ███ was arrested in January, the district started its own investigation into him. But ████████ County District Attorney ████████ asked it to stop while a grand jury investigated. The grand jury report is expected in a few weeks.

████████, a lawyer working on the investigation for the Long Island law firm of ████████ said she had an Aug. 12 letter from ████ saying that the district could now conduct any investigation it "deems appropriate." ████ was unavailable for comment.

████ confirmed that the investigation now includes questions about ███.

"The district is looking into a number of issues raised by faculty and others," she said. "We are trying to conduct a thorough investigation."

████ said there is no timetable for finishing the investigation, though she "hopes to conclude it in the near future."

████ said that at least two staff members were asked about ███ as late as yesterday. If the district wants to know who knew what about ███ it is asking the wrong people, Watkins said.

"At the end of the day, Cohen will be vindicated," he said. "And certain officials, including ████████ will have a lot to answer for."

████████ did not return a phone call seeking comment.

Behind The Schoolhouse Doors

Times Herald-Record Sunday, December 14, 2003

EDITORIALS - Michael K. Levine

The principal gets home work

The ███████ School District's probe of Bernard Cohen stinks.

It was like an early, and bad, April Fool's joke when the ███████ School District last March told employees of the high school that their principal, Bernard Cohen, was being investigated for taking petty cash, changing grades and assorted other matters that had nothing – *absolutely nothing*, mind you – to do with a sex scandal involving district superintendent ███████.

Cohen's lawyers called it nonsense. He called it retaliation. For our part, we thought it was a remarkable coincidence that a school board and district administrators who had been cited publicly by Cohen for failing to take timely and appropriate action on ███████ were all of a sudden investigating Cohen on unrelated administrative charges and making a public spectacle of it.

Of course, it turned out that all the skepticism was justified because, despite school officials' denials, the probe of Cohen soon veered from grades, petty cash and a hostile workplace to his handling of the ███████ issue. And last week, the district announced it had reassigned the principal to some vague duties to be done at home because, it says, he did not properly report his concerns about ███████'s relationship with a 14-year-old male high school student to school officials. An arbitrator will be asked to assess the charges.

The whole thing stinks to high heaven. We don't know if the district's claims about Cohen, regarding ███████ or anything else, have any merit, but the idea of a bunch of public officials, already the target of a grand jury probe for their own conduct in the ███████ affair, targeting another school employee, who undoubtedly testified against them to that grand jury, suggests a concerted effort to divert attention, legal and otherwise, from themselves.

To be credible, an investigation needs to be above suspicion. It needs to be handled objectively and without any hint of a predetermined outcome. It needs to be sponsored by an individual or individuals who have no personal stake in the outcome. It also needs to be conducted straightforwardly. ███████'s probe of Cohen fails on all those accounts.

As noted, it started with a false premise – that it had nothing to do with ███████. That bit of misdirection set it on a downward spiral. High school staff who were interviewed about Cohen by the investigators and who sat in on other staff interviews say the questioning was a "sham," that specific people were questioned to reach a specific outcome. And, of course, board members and district officials themselves are the subject of that grand jury inquiry, which included testimony from ███████.

Everything about the district probe suggests it is an effort to get Cohen. The thing is, even if Cohen warrants getting, the district probe is so weighted with conflicts and deceit, even an eventual arbitrator's decision that Cohen was negligent in dealing with ███████ will not necessarily convince a lot of people.

The former superintendent is in a state prison, having admitted to an improper sexual relationship with the youth. The district, however, is still in the throes of the fallout, with charges and countercharges about official accountability.

That puts considerable pressure where it belongs, on the probe being done by an ███████ County grand jury. One must presume these people have no stake in the outcome other than obtaining justice and that they will present the most detailed, accurate and credible picture of who did, or didn't do, what with regard to ███████.

234

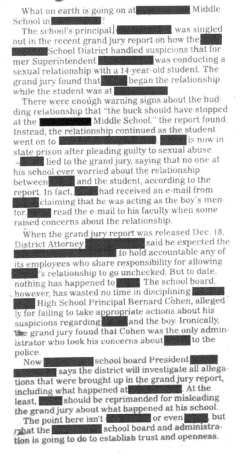

Times Herald-Record   Friday, January 2, 2004

EDITORIAL - Michael K. Levine

Actions in ▇▇▇▇ scandal don't inspire any trust

What on earth is going on at ▇▇▇▇▇ Middle School in ▇▇▇▇▇?

The school's principal ▇▇▇▇ was singled out in the recent grand jury report on how the ▇▇ ▇▇▇▇ School District handled suspicions that former Superintendent ▇▇▇▇▇ was conducting a sexual relationship with a 14-year-old student. The grand jury found that ▇▇▇ began the relationship while the student was at ▇▇▇▇

There were enough warning signs about the budding relationship that "the buck should have stopped at the ▇▇▇▇ Middle School," the report found. Instead, the relationship continued as the student went on to ▇▇▇▇▇▇▇▇▇ ▇▇▇ is now in state prison after pleading guilty to sexual abuse.

▇▇ lied to the grand jury, saying that no one at his school ever worried about the relationship between ▇▇ and the student, according to the report. In fact, ▇▇ had received an e-mail from ▇▇▇ claiming that he was acting as the boy's mentor. ▇▇ read the e-mail to his faculty when some raised concerns about the relationship.

When the grand jury report was released Dec. 18, District Attorney ▇▇▇▇▇ said he expected the ▇▇▇▇▇ to hold accountable any of its employees who share responsibility for allowing ▇▇▇'s relationship to go unchecked. But to date, nothing has happened to ▇▇▇ The school board, however, has wasted no time in disciplining ▇▇▇ High School Principal Bernard Cohen, allegedly for failing to take appropriate actions about his suspicions regarding ▇▇ and the boy. Ironically, the grand jury found that Cohen was the only administrator who took his concerns about ▇▇ to the police.

Now ▇▇▇▇ school board President ▇▇▇ ▇▇▇▇ says the district will investigate all allegations that were brought up in the grand jury report, including what happened at ▇▇▇▇ At the least, ▇▇ should be reprimanded for misleading the grand jury about what happened at his school.

The point here isn't ▇▇▇ or even ▇▇▇, but that the ▇▇▇ school board and administration is going to do to establish trust and openness.

Times Herald-Record   Tuesday, February 3, 2004

Cohen sues to get principal job back

By Jessica Gardner
Times Herald-Record

██ - Bernard Cohen wants his job back as principal of ██ High School.

The school board wants to fire him.

Cohen's lawyers filed a federal lawsuit Friday asking that a judge order district officials to stop singling him out for "retribution" and reinstate him as head of the high school.

The suit categorizes the district's actions against Cohen as a "Kafka-esque campaign of slander, intimidation and retaliation." It demands the district put an end to the disciplinary charges.

Cohen was reassigned to work at home in December after Acting Superintendent ██ filed disciplinary charges against him. The charges allege, among other things, that he failed to properly report his concerns about former Superintendent ██'s relationship with a male teenage student.

██ pleaded guilty to sodomy and is now serving a state prison sentence.

A grand jury report released a week after Cohen's reassignment found that Cohen was the only administrator to go to the police with concerns about the relationship.

"We were hopeful ... that once the report came out, the district would come to its senses," said Christopher Watkins, one of two lawyers representing Cohen. "Then we received notice last week that they were still going forward. That's when we decided to go to federal court."

██ a retired superintendent of the ██ School District in ██ County, took over for Cohen as principal on Jan. 1.

Cohen, who is still receiving full pay and benefits, has repeatedly said the disciplinary charges were filed as retaliation for his refusal to participate in a cover-up of the ██ scandal.

██ of ██ the Long Island firm acting as special labor counsel for the district, said Cohen ignored his legal obligation to make formal written reports of suspected child abuse.

"Maybe if he had done that, we wouldn't be where we are now," ██ said.

In addition to the district, defendants named in the lawsuit are ██ former school board member ██ school board President ██ Director of Special Services ██ and Deputy Superintendent ██

██ and ██ the lawyers who conducted the district's investigation, are also named in the suit.

██ denies any retaliation, saying, "The district is obligated to find out the truth regardless of the obstacles placed in our way."

The initial investigation into the high school was launched after the district received an anonymous letter claiming Cohen took petty cash and changed grades.

██ and ██ said the district's inquiry will now move on to ██ Middle School, central administration and the school board itself.

Times Herald-Recotrd Friday, July 23, 2004

Arbitrator bars ███████ report

Document can't be used as evidence in Cohen hearing

By Dianna Cahn
Times Herald-Record

████████ – The 50-page grand jury report into the ████ scandal can't be used as evidence in the case against suspended ████████ High School Principal Bernard Cohen, the arbitrator hearing his case ruled yesterday.

Arbitrator ████████ said the report, which is based on unnamed witness testimony, was hearsay, and he would rather rely on the testimony of witnesses appearing before him.

"You hired me to find a judgment based on this proceeding," said ████.

Yesterday was the second day of hearings into the district's case against Cohen. He faces five misconduct charges, among them that he failed to properly alert authorities to his suspicions that then-Superintendent ████████ was molesting a teenage student.

Cohen has maintained – and the grand jury report supports it – that he alerted the very officials who brought charges against him. He says the charges are their attempt to cover up their own failures to act against ████ who was later convicted and imprisoned.

████ was arrested in January 2003, and his deputy, ████ became acting superintendent. Within months, ████ began investigating anonymous allegations against Cohen, while the grand jury was conducting its own investigation into the ████ scandal.

Day two of the Cohen hearing, which continued from Monday, began with more testimony from ████████ assistant superintendent for business. ████ had participated in the Cohen investigation, monitoring "dozens" of interrogations of district staff.

████'s testimony said ████ confirmed hearing warnings about ████ from Cohen, but didn't give them credence because ████ knew Cohen and ████ didn't like each other.

████ said former school board President ████ told him Cohen had shown him a six-page memorandum. Cohen's lawyer, Chris Watkins, said the memo addressed Cohen's concerns about ████ District lawyer ████ said he believed the memo contained information about an unrelated topic.

████ and the district's second witness, ████, who is in charge of personnel for the district, both testified yesterday that they had seen the boy in ████'s office at the district on more than one occasion.

████ said he had warned ████ that it didn't look good. ████'s response?

"'It was sad,'" ████ recalled ████ saying, "'that in this day and age, someone can't help out a child, a student, without being accused of some kind of sexual interest.'"

████, meanwhile, agreed to allow defense questions into whether Cohen's supervisors had failed to act on suspicions about ████ The point could demonstrate Cohen was singled out unfairly.

████ said the district had not conducted any investigations into other officials.

████, who will rule on the charges and decide any penalties, scolded the lawyers.

It's a public hearing, he said.

"But I am not interested in either side making a record for public consumption out of this hearing.

"Frankly folks, you can air your dirty linen elsewhere."

Times Herald-Record photos/MICHAEL SPERLING
Suspended ████████ High School Principal Bernard Cohen and his lawyer, Chris Watkins, confer yesterday during Cohen's disciplinary proceedings. Among other things, the district accused Cohen of failing to properly alert authorities of a suspected sexual relationship between the former superintendent and a student.

Times Herald-Record   Monday, September 17, 2007

Full disclosure needed on Cohen settlement

Doug Cunningham

OPINION

We learn last week that there's been a settlement in the legal dispute between former ███████ High School Principal Bernie Cohen and the ████████ School District.

In classic school and legal bureaucratic fashion – a fashion that is understood only by those within this wacky cone of secrecy – we don't yet know how many hundreds of thousands of dollars this will cost the ███████ district. But you can bet it's a lot.

Perhaps – and I stress the word perhaps – we can now believe the inevitable assurances from the school district that it wants to move beyond the ███████ mess.

███████ is the molester who took advantage of his position to abuse a boy student in the district.

One of the very, very few people who sought to blow the whistle on ███'s predations was Cohen. Police finally busted ███ in 2003, and the unraveling of this sordid mess began.

As form follows in this district, the official response to Cohen's actions – undoubtedly steered and guided by the Board of Education – was to file trumped-up charges that he didn't make an "official" complaint regarding then-Superintendent ███ now a convicted molester. And, the district alleged, Cohen supposedly improperly changed Regents test scores. After a hearing, it fired him.

Cohen sued, seeking $6 million, saying the district was simply retaliating against him.

Me, I'm thinking he was about right on the mark. Cohen, I know, has his detractors. His style was not for everyone. But on this, he was right.

Just to recap, the thanks Cohen gets for sounding the alarm is to have his job placed in jeopardy. All the while, the district is spending money on legal fees as if the money spigot is broken and no one has a pliers.

It would be helpful now, lo these years later, if the district would actually wrap this up. It will not, for instance, be a sign the district wants to move on if it shrouds the cost of this settlement in secrecy.

This whole thing has been a debacle, not least for the victim. Full disclosure and thoughtful leadership at the beginning would have gone a long way toward setting things right a lot sooner.

APPENDIX A

TIMELINE OF EVENTS

My attorney, Chris Watkins, initially prepared this timeline as a summary overview for the Federal Judge. For this book, I have added several non-legal items relevant to the reader's full understanding of this complex story.

TIMELINE OF EVENTS

2000-2001: Superintendent Robert Parkman begins relationship with male eighth grade student, Seth, while Seth is a student in middle school.

Spring 2001: Bernard Cohen receives reports of concern about Parkman's relationship with Seth from Seth's Middle School teachers. Cohen asks Parkman about the relationship and Parkman claims he is "mentoring" Seth.

Spring 2001: Clearwater Board of Education raises concerns with Parkman about the relationship with Seth. He claims it is a "mentoring" relationship and BOE does not take any further action at that time.

Spring 2001: Cohen first reports concerns about the relationship to Clearwater police officer and School Resource Officer (SRO), Lieutenant Somerset, who advised Cohen he had received anonymous reports previously from Middle School staff members. Somerset tells Cohen that he does not want to place anything in writing for fear of leaks, given Parkman's high profile. Clearwater Police Department later confirms that Cohen first reported concerns about Parkman by at the latest June 2001.

July 2001: New York adopts "No Child Left Behind" which included a new required form for reporting abuse concerns.

September 2001: Seth enters Clearwater High School.

Fall 2001: Cohen continues to report concerns about Parkman's relationship to School Resource Officer Somerset. In addition, in November 2001, Cohen reports his concerns about the relationship to Deputy Superintendent, Ross. Ross does not take any action. According to Seth, and later Grand Jury report, Seth frequently visited Parkman in his office at the BOE building and they were alone in his office for hours at a time with the door closed. Ross' office was next door.

Fall 2001: BOE President Fletcher and Vice President Theresa Bradley speak with Parkman about his relationship with Seth. They have received reports that Parkman has been seen in his car with the boy and otherwise has been seen with the boy in the community. Fletcher and Theresa Bradley verbally warn Parkman to end relationship with Seth.

January 2002: Cohen speaks with Fletcher regarding his concerns about Parkman-Seth relationship. Fletcher advises Cohen that he and Theresa

Bradley are aware of concerns, have spoken with Parkman and will take additional action.

April 2002: Fletcher speaks with Cohen and school psychologist, Dr. Guevara, regarding their concerns about Parkman. Guevara tells Fletcher that he is concerned the relations may turn sexual. Fletcher later conceded that he knew at least from this point on, there was a possibility that the relationship might be "illicit."

April 30, 2002: With the assistance of School District's attorney, Fletcher and Theresa Bradley give Parkman secret letter directing him to cease all contact with Seth based on fact that relationship "is seen in many circles as inappropriate; at the worst, it is cause for speculation as to much more than that." Theresa Bradley later testified that letter was issued secretly and kept out of Parkman's personnel file so Parkman's future chances for employment would not be impaired.

May-June 2002: Parkman tells Ross that Board has given him a written directive to cease all contact with Seth. After this, Ross finds Parkman alone with Seth in the back of a Ruby Tuesday's restaurant. He testifies later that he felt "like I had walked in on something…Like it wasn't supposed to be happening. I had a very ugly feeling about this… it just made me very uncomfortable. I hated it." Ross did not report this incident to anyone other than to later testify.

July 2002: School Board elections result in the removal of Fletcher and other incumbents. Theresa Bradley becomes President of the Board. She was not running for the re-election. Only three of nine seats were up for election.

Summer 2002: The BOE extends Parkman's contract and gives him a raise.

September 2002: Seth transfers to Bedford High School, run by BOCES.

October 2002: Then BOE President Theresa Bradley issued Parkman a secret letter based on learning he had telephone contact with Seth. She writes that the letter is "not meant to be punitive"

January 8, 2003: The Clearwater P.D. arrests Parkman on charges of child sexual abuse. Seth had finally come forward to the police about the nature of their relationship and the P.D. caught Parkman making incriminating statements to Seth on authorized audiotape.

January 2003: The news media, particularly the local newspaper (*Times Herald-Record*), begins to investigate "who knew what and when" regarding Parkman's relationship with Seth.

The newspaper uncovers many damaging facts, including the secret letters that Fletcher and Theresa Bradley had issued to Parkman in 2002 regarding his relationship with Seth. The public is outraged at the daily revelations and a petition is circulated to recall the BOE. The BOE hires a lawyer to represent it in connection with the Parkman matter.

February 2003: The Orange County D.A. convenes a Grand Jury to investigate the School District and the D.A., publicly announces that criminal charges may ensue against School District.

February 2003: Through counsel, Cohen advises the BOE that he does not intend to assist it in covering up the truth regarding the Parkman matter. Cohen testifies at length to the Grand Jury in February and March 2003.

March 2003: Ross allegedly receives an anonymous letter at her house which accuses Cohen of stealing petty cash, changing grades for political favors and creating a hostile work environment. Seth later testifies that, before his arrest, Parkman had attempted to bring the same charges against Cohen, because he viewed Cohen as the biggest obstacle in continuing the relationship. Parkman later partially confirms this at his deposition from prison.

April 1, 2003: Without any notice to Cohen, Ross and BOE President Theresa Bradley convene a faculty and staff meeting at the High School. Ross announces that Cohen is under investigation based on allegations that he stole from petty cash, changed grades for political favors and created a hostile work environment. These allegations make the newspaper the next day.

April 2, 2003: In response, Cohen goes public regarding what Ross and others, including the BOE, knew about the Parkman-Seth relationship and why they would be trying to attack him.

April-December 2003: Ross and the BOE conduct a nine-month investigation of Cohen looking for evidence of misconduct. The investigation costs the District over $100,000.

July 2003: Parkman pleads guilty to sodomy of a minor and is sentenced to state prison.

December 9, 2003: Ross proffers five charges against Cohen approved by the BOE. The first is for failure to make a written report regarding concerns about Parkman's relationship with Seth. The second charge specifies that Cohen failed to properly denote changes made to Regents Test scores. The third though fifth charges concern staffing of a GED English class and the IEP of a particular student. Cohen is placed on paid suspension.

December 19, 2003: The Orange County Grand Jury issues a public report which excoriates the School District in connection with Parkman and Seth, noting a "complete breakdown of the leadership components" that "resulted in the failure to protect the student." Although the report omits names, it singles out Cohen (by position) as the only administrator to report Parkman to the police and who sounded the alarm within the School District.

2004-2005: A 3020-A Competency Hearing is held on the charges against Cohen. The Hearing Officer refuses to allow into evidence the Grand Jury report and refuses to allow Cohen to defend against the charges on the ground that they are all retaliatory for his First Amendment-protected speech. The Hearing Officer finds Cohen guilty of the first and second charge(s) and he is terminated in August 2005.

May 2005: Cohen files a federal lawsuit against the District and several officials for First Amendment retaliation.

September 2005: Cohen initiates an appeal of the Hearing Officer's decision.

September 2007: After two years of discovery, the District settles Cohen's federal lawsuit for $425,000. Cohen must agree to drop his appeal of the 3020-A decision. As a result of dropping his appeal of the Competency Hearing result, the State Education Department removes Cohen's education licenses.

APPENDIX B

This appendix shows the email written by the Superintendent to the staff of Seth's Middle School several of whom had already started to report Parkman's inappropriate behavior to their administration. The references in parentheses are pages of testimony transcripts.

These paragraphs speak to the Middle School teachers' and counselors' willingness to protest the Superintendent's behavior and Parkman's response to them.

Tuesday, June, 05, 2001 11:14:20AM
Message

From: ▮▮▮▮▮▮▮▮
Subject: ▮▮▮▮▮▮▮▮
To: ▮▮▮▮▮▮▮▮

Word has gotten around that some teachers in your building are discussing my association with ▮▮▮. While I try to be thick-skinned about most issues that come to me either professionally or personally, this matter is distressing. *My hope is that you will share this note with those who may be inclined to question my relationship with this student.*

I do not apologize or hide the fact that I have been mentoring this child for the last several months, and have on occasion bought him clothes and have had him as a guest in my home. My association with ▮▮▮ has been nothing less than public in all regards, and those who are acquainted with this boy surely understand the needs he has. I have had the pleasure of counseling him on a number of issues, including his academic achievement, school attendance, family issues, social behavior, his speech, and personal hygiene (last week I bought him a bottle of shampoo, deodorant, and toothpaste – and told him how to use each).

I do this of my free will, and with full knowledge and consent of his parents. I'm sure you're aware that occasionally many of us (educators) encounter students in our lives for whom we give a little extra. We "dress an angel," provide scholarship money, contribute a pair of shoes or a winter coat, school supplies, etc. etc. I am happy that I can help wherever possible. I also personally provide an annual scholarship at ███, and have privately provided financial assistance to other students in this district – no differently than you, and many of our colleagues.

I have asked (told) ███ that he is not to "use" this association with me. However, rambunctious 13-year old that he is, I'm aware that he has exploited his acquaintance with me for his personal gains. We have discussed this and expect it will not continue. On one occasion, a few months ago, ███ father called me with an issue that I spoke to ███ about. Together we were able to resolve the matter. Afterward, I admonished ███ that he had spent a rather large favor in asking for my intervention. While he whines about school as anyone does, he has not asked me to intervene since then.

My association with ███ █ is not without my own personal enjoyment. When he is with my family and me, ███ is energetic, (sometimes off the wall!), helpful, inquisitive, friendly, and polite. I am not unaware of this child's defects academically, psychologically, or socially. Similarly, I am not unaware of this kids' potential and this concomitant strengths. I have related my association with ███ to the board, describing him as my "starfish." (You know the parable.). I don't deny the good feelings in being able to help ███ with some of his issues. I'm sure we're all grateful for the good fortune to assist others less able than we are.

I expect that my relationship with this child can be viewed with the honesty and openness it deserves. Moreover, I hope you will let me know additional ways in which I might be of service to you in assisting him. Thank you for the opportunity to make this explanation.

Excerpt from Bernard H. Cohen's Post-Hearing Brief prepared by Chris Watkins relevant to the Superintendent's email:

Middle School Principal also denied having spoken with Cohen about the issue in 2001, (see Tr. 645-46), but according to Cohen, he spoke with the Middle School Principal in spring 2001. (Tr. 1773). Cohen ask the Middle School Principal if what he had been hearing was accurate, namely that ███████ was having daily in-person and telephone contact with ██, and intervening on the boy's behalf at school. (Tr. 1773-76). ██████ corroborated the accuracy of this information. (Tr. 1776). When Cohen suggested that ██████ needed to take some action to protect the boy, ██████ responded that Cohen was crazy and that he could not tell the Superintendent what to do. (Tr. 1777).

On or about June 5, 2001, at ████████'s behest, ██████ read an e-mail from ████████ to staff and faculty defending ████████'s relationship with ██. (Rx O; Tr. 648, 653). The first sentence of the e-mail reads: "word has gotten around that some teachers in your building are discussing my association with ██." (Rx O). The e-mail is a disturbing *apologia* for an illicit, abusive relationship with an 8th grade student (Rx O). Under the circumstances, it is reasonable to infer that ████████ directed ██████ to read the e-mail to intimidate faculty and staff from raising concerns about ████████'s inappropriate relationship with ██. (Rx O). ██████ denies that, by reading ████████'s e-mail, he might be suppressing staff and faculty from raising concerns (Tr. 654-55).

APPENDIX C

This appendix is a direct copy of the guidelines that were in place when I first went to the police with my concerns. Although, it was pointless to report any concerns to the Superintendent, I did as the guidelines required. I also reported to the Superintendent's designee for sexual abuse, but was turned away "because you're after his job and I'm not getting caught in-between the two of you."

REGULATION	1998	5460R 1 of 2
	Students	

SUBJECT: CHILD ABUSE INVOLVING SCHOOL PERSONNEL

The Enlarged City School District designates the school principal in each building to be responsible to accept, investigate, document, and report to the Superintendent or designee, suspected cases of child abuse involving school personnel.

Any person receiving information about alleged child abuse shall immediately report that information to the school building principal or a designated representative when the principal is unavailable who will immediately notify the Superintendent or designee and the school attorney.

In order to safeguard the rights and reputation of all individuals, it is understood that the reporting, documentation, and investigation will be conducted in a confidential manner. Any conversations with the employee will be held in a private setting.

The principal and the Superintendent's designee are authorized to conduct interviews of appropriate staff and/or student(s) to ascertain the facts in the case. They will document the reported facts in writing. If there is a visible trauma, color photographs will be taken at District expense.

The principal and the Superintendent's designee will report the findings to the Superintendent who will, in turn, inform the President of the Board of Education (without specifying the name of the person unless continuation of the investigation is warranted) and the school attorney. The principal will inform the parents and request a conference in the school. When there is serious doubts that any crime has been committed, the Superintendent or designee will review the case with the school attorney before deciding on closure. Written reports of the investigation including a summary of the results, and the reasons no action was taken will be kept by the Superintendent in a sealed file in his or her office for a period of five years and then expunged.

If the principal determines that there is a threat to the child's health or safety, the Superintendent will consider the immediate removal of the accused from direct student contact provided that such removal shall not continue beyond the date of the next meeting of the Board of Education unless appropriate charges are preferred against the suspect employee at such meeting.

If, during or at the conclusion of the investigation, there is responsible grounds to believe the allegations, the principal will follow the procedures outlined below.

1) The principal will immediately notify the Superintendent or designee who will call the District Attorney's office and ask for a responsible individual to whom he/she may report an incident of child abuse.

(Continued)

Bernard H. Cohen

SUBJECT: CHILD ABUSE INVOLVING SCHOOL PERSONNEL (Cont'd.)

2) The principal will immediately report the incident to the appropriate law enforcement agency. When reporting to the police, the principal should ask for a responsible individual to whom he/she may report an incident of child abuse.

3) The principal will forward reports of the investigation along with a summary of the results to the Personnel Office for inclusion in the employee's personnel file and Personnel shall provide a copy to the employee.

In the event that it is established by the school administration that an employee has committed acts which raise reasonable questions as to improper or unprofessional conduct by said individual, the Superintendent shall take the following actions:

1) Professional staff shall be reported, in accordance with Part 83 of the rules and regulations of the Commissioner of Education, to the Director of Teacher Education and Certification. In addition, appropriate disciplinary proceedings pursuant to Section 3020-A shall be activated, where applicable.

2) Non-instructional employees shall be reported to the appropriate governmental agency responsible for civil service personnel. In addition, appropriate disciplinary proceedings pursuant to Section 75 of the Civil Service Law shall be activated, where applicable.

The District will identify appropriate school personnel to participate in awareness instruction and training with respect to receiving or obtaining information regarding the circumstances surrounding the identification of child abuse.

To the extent permitted by law, individuals reporting suspected child abuse in good faith shall be immune from civil or criminal liability that might otherwise arise.

APPENDIX D

GRAND JURY REPORT

After Parkman was arrested, the District Attorney used the Grand Jury process to indict the Superintendent. When Parkman was sentenced, the same Grand Jury then heard testimony regarding "who knew what when." I have only included pages of the Grand Jury Report that add dimension and/or further clarify aspects of this case that comprise my part of this story. Much of the total report is a redundant review of District Training activities related to sexual abuse reporting and employee lack of reporting.

The Grand Jury Report blames the non-reporting of Parkman on poor training. In my opinion, the District's Personnel Director did an outstanding job in this regard. Those staff interviewed by the Grand Jury blamed the training because they would otherwise have to blame themselves.

In addition, the Grand Jury Report reviews the District's reporting guidelines but fails to address the fact that procedures require

Principals to report such concerns to the Superintendent. They make no suggestions for reporting if the alleged perpetrator *is* the Superintendent. The guidelines, shown in a later Appendix, state that a Principal or other administrator should report sexual abuse concerns to the Superintendent, the Police and the School Board President, all of which I did. The Board President finally admitted that several in addition to me reported concerns to him, the Police testified that I was the only person who reported to the Police.

██████████████████████ **COURT GRAND JURY**

NOVEMBER 21, 2003

GRAND JURY REPORT, CPL 190.85 (1) (C)

"evils that befall the world are not nearly so often caused by bad men as they are good men who are silent when an opinion must be voiced."[1]

PREMLIMINARY STATEMENT

The ████████████████████ Grand Jury, Term 1, was empanelled on January 6, 2003 by the order of the Honorable ████████████████, County Court Judge.[2]

… The Grand Jury heard testimony from 81 witnesses covering nearly 4,000 pages of testimony and considered 70 exhibits, many consisting of multiple pages and documents.[3] All those who testified before this Grand Jury receive immunity from any criminal prosecution that may have resulted from testimony elicited during this investigation into the ████████████████████████ School District…

I.   INTRODUCTION/OVERVIEW

…The hierarchy of the school system consists of a nine-member school board that votes on policy, contractual, budgetary and other school related issues. All members of the School Board are volunteers and elected by the public. The School Board has a President and a Vice-President… During testimony by board members it became clear that during executive sessions not all board members remembered what items were discussed. Also during testimony heard by this Grand Jury it became evident that not all Board members were apprised of all the facts surrounding the day-to-day affairs of the District. This included a so-called "disciplinary action" taken by one member of the Board in regards to the school official's mentoring relationship with a student. Letters, memos and e-mails that were written to and from certain Board members and the school official were never shared with the other Board members until after the criminal arrest of the school official.

...The Grand Jury also heard testimony in reference to the Education Law[7] in respect to the requirements that teachers, administrators, school nurses, guidance counselors, school psychologists, school social workers, School Board members and all other school personnel required to hold a teaching or administrative license or certification must follow in the event of suspected child abuse. This law established a reporting process that must be followed. When these employees receive an allegation of child abuse by an employee or volunteer in an educational setting, they must take the following steps:

A) Upon receiving an oral or written allegation of child abuse occurring in an educational setting, the employee must promptly complete a written form detailing the facts surrounding the allegation.

B) After completion of that form the employee must personally deliver the completed form to the school building administrator of the school in which the alleged abuse occurred...

...If reasonable suspicion is found an administrator must take steps which may differ depending upon the individual who had made the allegation. In all cases the parent of the child must be notified of the alleged abuse and the appropriate law enforcement agency must receive a copy of the completed form.

II.   THE FUNCTION AND PURPOSE OF CHILD PROTEC-TIVE SERVICES AT THE COUNTY AND STATE LEVEL

...Child Protective Services is a division of the Department of Social Services and has the primary legal responsibility to investigate allegations of abuse and neglect made against a parent, guardian, or other person legally responsible for a child.

...In New York, "mandatory reporters" are recognized as a certain group of professionals that are specially equipped, by their formal training and experience, to hold this important role. Common examples of mandatory reporters are physicians, law enforcement officials[9], teachers, childcare workers and mental health professionals.

...The central function of the Child Protective Service is two-fold. First and foremost, Child Protective Service (C.P.S.) exists to protect children from harm inflicted on them by individuals who are legally responsible for them. Second, while ever mindful of their responsibility to keep children safe, C.P.S. is required and strives to restore or enable family functioning and to keep families together, if possible. Thus C.P.S. has no legal responsibility to investigate cases involving children who have been abused by a legal stranger, including priests, teachers, or any other adult who is not a parent, guardian or person legally responsible for the child.

Similarly, abuse alleged to have been committed by someone, other than the parent, guardian or other person responsible for the child, is not the proper subject of a report to the State Central Registry hotline... C.P.S. conducts no investigations into these cases.

III. THE RELATIONSHIP WITH A SCHOOL EMPLOYEE

During the course of the Grand Jury's investigation of the ███████ ██████████████ School District, it became clear to members of the Grand Jury that a student enrolled within the School District developed a strong, personal relationship with a high-ranking school official. The relationship eventually became a sexual relationship.

The Grand Jury heard and fully credits testimony received from the minor child involved in this case after comparing and contrasting that testimony with other witnesses who testified before the Grand Jury...

Testimony was heard that a student enrolled in the ██████████ School District first met and became friends with a high-ranking school official during the 1999/2000 school year. The relationship between the student and the school official started when the student went to see the official about a problem he was having at the ██████ ████████ Middle School. From the first meeting it is very clear the school official and the student were interested in each other's company. During the first meeting, the high-ranking school official invited the student to visit the official at the ███████████ Board of Education building. The student quickly took up this offer.

The Grand Jury learned that over the course of the next two and one-half years, the student's relationship with the school official grew stronger and closer. The evidence shows that the student visited the school official at the Board of Education building up to thirty (30) times over the school years of 2000-2002…

The Grand Jury heard the evidence that demonstrated the extensive access the student had to confidential School District documents. The evidence showed that the student was frequently allowed to deliver documents, files, school reports, discipline reports, teacher's evaluation, school contracts, and other confidential material to other school employees within the Board of Education building. The student freely related to the Grand Jury how the student read those documents and then confronted District employees with the student's knowledge of the documents in order to intimidate District employees. The student learned and knew confidential material. At times, the student discussed these very matters with the school official whom the student came to visit.

The Grand Jury heard testimony that, on numerous occasions, the school official and the student visited pornographic websites together using the School District's Internet access. After visiting these websites, the school official would ask the student to remove any evidence from the computer showing these pornographic sites…

It became evident to the Grand Jury that as time passed, the student and the school official became more closely involved.

The school official took the student to school functions with him and purchased for the student numerous gifts. These gifts first started out as minor personal items, but came to include clothing, shoes, computer-related items[11], and items for the student's other family members.

The school official invited the student to the official's home. The student accepted these invitations and visited the school official's home often during the period of time 2000-2002...

Sometimes during the years of 2000-2002, the high-ranking school official and the student developed a sexual relationship...

...The school official used intimidation and deceit in order to strengthen his relationship with the student. One school faculty member, who was untenured[12], testified that the school official actually visited the faculty member's classroom while in session, because the student had complained to the school official about the faculty member...

We find that at the end of April 2002, the school official received a letter[13] from a School Board member, which the Grand Jury concluded was a letter of reprimand. It stated in substance that the school official must "CEASE" and "DESIST" all further contact with the student. Testimony was given that the school official acknowledged the letter and signed it. A copy of the letter was to be placed in the school official's personnel folder and in a file at a law firm that handles the District's legal work.

The Grand Jury subpoenaed the personnel files of the school official and found no such letter...Testimony received by the Grand Jury revealed that other school administrators in the School District were aware of this letter, but the school official still continued to see the student regularly.

We find that during the month of September 2002, the school official via e-mail[14] sent a Board member a memo dated 9/26/02, in which the school official freely acknowledged that he had had contact with the student by telephone. Evidence showed that, as a result of this memo, the Board member issued a second letter of reprimand ordering the school official to stop any contract with this child. The school official signed the second letter. The memo, like the previous memo, indicated that a copy was to be placed in the school official's personnel file and in a file maintained by the law firm. The Grand Jury found no such letter in the school official's file. Instead, the Grand Jury received a copy of that letter from the same law firm that handles the District's legal work. The testimony before the Grand Jury revealed that this second letter of reprimand was never shown to or discussed with other Board members until after the school official's arrest.

In the Fall 2002, after the second letter of reprimand had been sent to, and acknowledged by, the school official, the Board voted to extend the school official's contract[15] with a raise included. Also in the Fall 2002, the student was transferred to an alternative school administered by BOCES...

IV. TEACHERS IN THE ███████████ SCHOOL DISTRICT AND TRAINING RELATED TO THE RECOGNIZING AND REPORTING OF CHILD ABUSE

...The Grand Jury found most disturbing the conflicts in testimony from the teachers and staff members as to what training and direction they received from the School District in reference to recognizing and reporting child abuse in a school setting. This Grand Jury was unable to reconcile the testimony of the teachers with that of the individuals in charge of training in responses to questions regarding training on recognizing and reporting child abuse...

The Grand Jury found the testimony of the School District staff members in conflict with the testimony elicited from the people directing training with regard to yearly training on child abuse. However, nothing was more perplexing to the Grand Jury than when the Grand Jury compared the training sign-in logs with witnesses who testified before the Grand Jury. When comparing the sexual abuse training sign-in logs with the witnesses who testified, the Grand Jury found many of the witnesses who testified before the Grand Jury had in fact received training on the subject within the District.[20]...

V. WHAT DID SCHOOL EMPLOYEES AT ████ ████ KNOW AND SEE

...The Grand Jury finds that the relationship between the school official and the student first started at the ████ ████ Middle School, and with the proper intervention, could have been stopped. As a result of this investigation, the Grand Jury finds that employees in authority at the School District could have and should have prevented the events that eventually unfolded in the ████ ████ School District. In other terms, the buck should have stopped at ████ ████ Middle School.

One middle school administrator, who appeared before this Grand Jury, testified he first met the student in September 1998... According to the administrator's testimony, no one at the Middle School expressed any concern about the relationship between the school official and the student. Yet the Grand Jury finds that in June 2001, an administrator of the Middle School read an e-mail[22] that was sent to him by the school official and also to the faculty members at ███████ ███████ during a faculty gathering in order to answer their concerns about the relationship. The Grand Jury finds that after hearing the testimony from other staff members at the ███████ ███████ Middle School, the Middle School administrator was well aware of the concerns the faculty had with the relationship. The Middle School administrator testified that there is no written policy on the mentoring process that he was aware of... The administrator also testified that he had instructed the faculty not to remove students from school in their personal vehicles, yet he testified that the school official would pick up the student and the student's sibling everyday from school and drive them home.

...The testimony clearly showed that the school failed to follow its own policy with regards to students being removed from their classrooms.

VI. WHAT DID SCHOOL EMPLOYEES AT THE HIGH SCHOOL KNOW AND SEE

...During the course of the investigation, it became quite evident to the members of the Grand Jury that ███████ High School administrators, faculty and staff were well aware of a relationship between the school official and a student en-rolled at the ███████████ High School. Many administra-tors, faculty and staff members believed it to be an inappropri-ate mentoring relationship.

High school administrators testified that, on numerous occa-sions, the school official requested special treatment and favors for the student. Testimony revealed that during the beginning weeks of the school semester 2001 to 2002, the faculty and staff informed the High School administrators that the school official had signed the student in late approximately forty (40) times during the first semester. As noted before, the school official also signed the student out numerous times from detention.[25]

One administrator testified that he went to see a member of the School Board at the Board member's personal business, to advise him of concerns that administrators and faculty had regarding the school official's relationship with the student. The administrator advised the School Board member that the relationship between the school official and the student in-volved gift-giving, as well as spending time at the school offi-cial's home on weekdays and weekends.

Through the course of the ninth grade school year, an ad-ministrator of the High School also advised several other peo-ple within the School District of the concerns of the faculty and staff, including a member of the School Board. An administra-tor testified that he advised two high-ranking administrators, a police officer and a lawyer that represents the school adminis-trators. The administrator testified before the Grand Jury that he told another administrator and others involved in the edu-cational field that "if he (the school official) is not in the boy's pants now, he soon will be." In response, one senior administrator suggested there was nothing that could be done, based upon the school official's position in the District....

...Several faculty members testified that they were concerned about the relationship between the student and the school official. However, they further testified that they believed that administration and law enforcement officials were handling this problem...

...A police officer testified that he was made aware of the relationship involving a student and the school official in the beginning of September 2001. Thereafter, an administrator at the school spoke with the police officer at least once a week about the student, explaining his concerns...

VII. **WHAT DID SCHOOL EMPLOYEES AT THE BOARD OF EDUCATION KNOW AND SEE**

This Grand Jury heard testimony from a broad spectrum of School District employee, including the administrators, professional and support staff.

Several school employees testified before the Grand Jury that they were aware of a relationship between the school official and a student enrolled in the ███████ ███████ School District. In fact, witnesses testified that they had seen the student inside the Board of Education building several times with the school official...

...One witness advised the Grand Jury that she became aware of a letter[28] written by a School Board member reprimanding the school official for his relationship with the student. The school official told her that the letter stated that the school official was no longer to have any contact with the student. Yet, this same administrator testified that she was out on a luncheon with other faculty members at a local eatery in the ███████████ area, and saw the school official with the student at a restaurant. This sighting occurred after she became aware of the letter of reprimand. The administrator testified that she felt embarrassed and that she knew the school official was not supposed to be with the student. The school administrator never reported what she saw to anyone...

...The Grand Jury heard testimony from several witnesses regarding the school official's improper use of school computers...On one occasion, a school employee was working on the school official's computer and came across a photograph (that was attached to an instant messenger buddy name) of a male (the head and bottom legs were cropped off) exposing his genitals. The worker notified his superior, but the supervisor merely ordered the worker to delete the image. Although the supervisor testified he felt the photograph was inappropriate, the supervisor never confronted the school official about the photograph or mentioned it to anyone else...

...The Grand Jury heard other testimony from witnesses who had seen the student in the Board office a number of times. The evidence demonstrated that the student was at liberty to walk around the Board building alone, and that at times the student was alone in the school official's office where confidential files are kept. The testimony made clear that the student was allowed special status at the Board of Education building, and was an interruptive, if not disruptive, presence at the building...

VIII. **WHAT THE SCHOOL BOARD KNEW AND DID**

...The evidence demonstrated that certain Board members had been alerted to the alleged improprieties and had even become involved in the sanctioning of the school official through two separate "Cease and Desist" letters. Yet, these same individuals failed to share this important information with the rest of the Board, despite the fact that the School Board was considering (and eventually ratified), the school official's contract extension. In addition, certain Board members discussed the improper relationship between the school official and the student with the attorneys who were hired to represent the School Board. The attorneys assisted in drafting the "Cease and Desist" letters, and maintained copies of those letters in files maintained at the law firm. The lawyers who represented the School Board also represented ███████████████ BOCES.

Ultimately, the Grand Jury finds that certain Board members either knew or suspected an improper relationship, but either failed to act or acted unilaterally. More importantly, the Grand Jury can only conclude that the failure of certain Board members to share pertinent and relevant information with the remaining Board member enabled the school official to continue his relationship with the student, virtually unchecked.

IX. **WHAT BOCES KNEW AND DID**

...The Grand Jury quickly learned from the testimony of an ███████████████ BOCES employee that late in the 2001-2002 school year, an employee of ███████████

BOCES was informed by several sources of the possible improper relationship between a ██████████ School District employee and a high school student. The ████████ █████ BOCES employee immediately became suspicious that a pedophilic relationship may exist between the ██████████ School District employee and a high school student.

Upon receiving the information, the ████████ █████ BOCES employee took three courses of action. First, the employee called the ██████████ School District and inquired about the matter. The employee was told that the ██████████ School District had already handled the matter. The testimony before the Grand Jury further revealed that the ████████ ██████ BOCES employee then contacted the State Board of Education Professional Ethics Section for advice on the matter, at which time the employee claims he was informed that ████████ █████ BOCES lacked the investigative power to look into this matter. The Grand Jury also heard from a member of the State Board of Education, whose testimony showed that this information was clearly erroneous. The State Board of Education official informed the Grand Jury that the ████████ ██████ BOCES could look into the matter if necessary, since BOCES did have general power to investigate School Districts while acting under the power of the Commissioner of Education.

Further testimony by a BOCES employee revealed that a BOCES employee contacted legal counsel and asked for advice on how to handle the matter. The Grand Jury learned through testimony that the legal counsel the BOCES employee contacted was the same legal counsel used by the ██████████ School District as general counsel. Thus, when a member of

██████████████████ BOCES contacted their legal counsel, they learned that legal counsel was already aware of the situation. However, counsel could not give any advice, other than the matter was being handled, due to a legal conflict of interest.

Through testimony the Grand Jury also learned a member of BOCES personally called the involved ██████████████ School District official and spoke with him about the matter in mid-2002. It appears to the Grand Jury that the school official assured the BOCES employee that any relationship between a student and the school official was purely a mentoring relationship.

After examining and comparing and contrasting the testimony of BOCES employees, ██████████████ School District employees, the legal counsel of both entities and a member from the State Department of Education, the Grand Jury can only conclude that this is yet another example of the continuing failure of the educational system to take the appropriate actions. The testimony before the Grand Jury shows that, upon first impression, at least one BOCES employee thought the relationship was pedophilic in nature and shared this fear with others, and yet no substantive action was taken.

X. RECOMMENDATIONS

...this Grand Jury recommends copies of this report be forwarded to every employee within the ██████████████████████ School District as well as the current School Board members. Copies of this report should also be made available to the citizens of ████████ County, in particular, those residents of the ██████████████████████ School District.

APPENDIX E

SUSPENSION LETTER FROM DISTRICT

After calling me in to headquarters and suspending me, I received the letter in this appendix, along with homework assignments.

School District
New York

Acting Superintendent of Schools

Mr. Bernard Cohen

Piermont, NY 10968

December 10, 2003

Dear Mr. Cohen,

This letter follows our meeting on December 10, 2003 at which time I informed you that you are hereby reassigned to home to perform the duties listed on the attached letter, effective immediately. Your salary, fringe benefits, tenure status, tenure area, and other terms and conditions of employment will remain unchanged except as specified in this letter or by future directive.

Prior to entering upon school grounds for any employment-related reason, you are required to obtain approval from myself or Deputy Superintendent ███████ At our meeting, I asked you to return all District property and informed you that arrangements are being made for you to pick up any personal items at the school. If you require further access to District property, equipment, or personnel in order for you to properly perform your assigned duties, then you are advised to inform ██████████ or myself as soon as you become aware of this need.

During your reassignment, you are directed not to contact school district employees, students or parents in your capacity as a ████████ School District employee, except to the extent that this is necessary for you to properly perform your assignments. In this case, you are still required to seek prior approval.

At our meeting, you were also given the opportunity to ask questions about the scope, nature, and meaning of the directives. Again, I encourage you to notify me as soon as possible if you have any further questions.

Sincerely,

Acting Superintendent of Schools

12/10/03

Signature acknowledges that I have received, read, understand and will comply with this letter.

APPENDIX F

REMOVAL OF MY EDUCATION LICENSES DUE TO QUESTION OF MORAL CHARACTER

After being the only person to report the Superintendent to Police and also report those who did nothing when I brought them my concerns, those same people had the power to fire me "for not reporting." I reported verbally but did not file written reports because the police directed me to put nothing in writing.

This appendix is page one of the letter I received demanding I submit my licenses for revocation. I gladly turned in my licenses to a State Education Department so corrupt that they based this decision on a lack of Federal adjudication. I settled out of court. Had I gone to court and won, the State would not have revoked the licenses. I chose to take the settlement and move on rather than go back to work in that District.

The University of the State of New York
Education Department

In the matter of a proceeding held
pursuant to 8 NYCRR Part 83, to
determine whether

BERNARD H. COHEN

has the requisite good moral character
to teach in the public schools of the
State of New York

**NOTICE OF SUBSTANTIAL
QUESTION OF MORAL
CHARACTER**

  BERNARD H. COHEN, hereinafter referred to as "certificate holder", presently holds

the following permanent New York State certificates: as a Reading Teacher, effective

September 1, 1988; as a School Administrator and Supervisor, effective September 1, 1988; and

as a School District Administrator, effective September 1, 1989. Each certificate bears the

number ███████

  Information has been received by the New York State Education Department that on or

about August 22, 2005, certificate holder was found guilty, after a hearing held pursuant to

Education Law 3020-a, of the following:

1) Failing to make one or more mandatory reports regarding knowledge and/or belief

  about a relationship between the Superintendent of Schools and a male student.

2) Compromising the validity of the June 2002 ███████ Regents Examination by,

  among other things: a) changing student grades, b) changing one or more student

  examination scores without entering his initials in the boxes next to the questions

  scored and changed and c) changing the scaled scores of one or more students from a

  failing grade to a passing grade without noting any increase in the student's credit

APPENDIX G

LETTER FROM BOARD OF EDUCATION PRESIDENT TO SUPERINTENDENT

The following letter was prepared only after ten of the high school teachers threatened to speak publicly about Parkman at the next School Board meeting.

President of the Board of Education

April 30, 2002

Superintendent of Schools

Re: Personal Conduct

Dear ▆▆▆:

It grieves me to have to write this letter to you in my capacity as President of the Board of Education.

As you already know, it has come to my attention that you have engaged in a pattern of conduct with a male student who is currently a freshman at the high school. This conduct included interacting with him privately, breakfast and lunch meetings, transporting him in your vehicle, purchasing personal items, and from time to time, removing him from school.

Most recently, you have intervened in varied disciplinary actions consequent to his behavior at the high school. In previous conversations regarding this matter, you have been made aware of the fact that while the intent may be pure, the perception is not. We have discussed the fact that various members of the community, both within the schools as well as in the community at large, view the relationship with this student with concern. At the least, it is seen in many circles as inappropriate; at the worst, it is cause for speculation as to much more than that.

I have voiced a concern that the whole series of incidents put both you and the District that you represent as the Superintendent, in a compromised position. We have discussed the need to distance yourself from this situation. I am writing at this time to re-enforce that need. If you continue in this relationship, and the public becomes more aware of the situation, it could cause irreparable damage to you personally, to your family and to the institution that your serve so conscientiously.

As President of the Board of Education, I am directing that you take immediate steps to cease and desist from any further contact with this student, in any form whatsoever. The Board will be apprised of this directive in a timely and appropriate manner. If this directive is violated, please be informed that such action will be viewed as a disciplinary infraction, and the Board will act accordingly.

This correspondence will be kept on file with our attorney, ██████ ███████████, indefinitely. It is my hope that the Board of Education will never find the need to refer to it in the future.

This document has been reviewed with you by me personally, in the context of a conference call with Mr. ███████████, on the 30th of April 2002.

Sincerely,

███████ █ ████████, ████
President of the Board of Education
███████ ████████
████████ ██████████████

APPENDIX H

The following is one page of the boy's statement regarding the Superintendent's plan to fire me.

1   A   Yes.

2   Q   Did ███ ever tell you that on any other

3 occasion, besides that occasion you just told us

4 about?

5   A   Every single time I told him Cohen asked

6 me.

7   Q   He said that Cohen was trying to break the

8 two of you up?

9   A   And get his job, yes.

10   Q   Did ███ ever tell you that he wanted to

11 get Mr. Cohen fired?

12   A   Yes.

13   Q   When was the first time ███ told you

14 that?

15   A   Probably in the Fall.

16   Q   Fall of what year?

17   A   My ninth grade year.

18   Q   What were the circumstances of ███

19 telling you that?

20   A   Well, he said that Mr. Cohen was a fat

21 fuck.

22   Q   What else did he say?

23   A   He said that he was trying to break us up

24 and he was trying to cause ███ trouble, and that

25 ███ was going to have him thrown out on his fat

APPENDIX I

MEMO PRESENTED BY BERNARD COHEN TO SCHOOL BOARD PRESIDENT

The following memo summarized Bernard Cohen's observations of the Superintendent's behaviors that caused Cohen to report his concerns to police, the School Board President, and others.

To: ████████████

From: Bernard H. Cohen

Date: May 6, 2002

Subj: Superintendent's Relationship with a student

Prior to the start of the current school year (2001-2002), Superintendent ██████████████ told me of his relationship with a middle school student attending ██████ ███████ Middle School. It was approximately half-way through the school year (2000-2001) when Mr. ████████ informed me about a young boy named ████, with who he had started a "mentoring relationship". Mr. ████████ told me that the boy had serious attendance problems at ████████ ████████ Middle School. His principal, Mr. ████████ ██████, used various motivational techniques with the boy to improve attendance. At one point, Mr. ██████ had asked ██████ to identify something reasonable that ██████ could be given as a gift for perfect attendance over a two-week period. The Superintendent told me that Mr. ██████ responded positively to ███ when ██████ said, "If I come to school for two-weeks without any absences, I want to be introduced to the Superintendent of Schools." Apparently, this resulted in ████████, two weeks later, donning a suit and visiting the Superintendent's office. Mr. ████████ informed me that he was "immediately impressed with the boys' manners and mannerisms that seemed right out of a European high culture."

For the remainder of school year 2000-2001, although I never met ██████, I was regaled with stories about ██████ every time I visited the Superintendent's office. During the Spring term of that school year, I generally visited the Superintendent weekly for one reason or another or we spoke on the phone, the latter of which might have occurred several times per week. Without exception, especially if I visited Mr. ███████'s office alone, I always heard at least one story about ██████'s talents, behavior, technological awarenesses, clothing, family issues or other aspects of██████'s life.

After several months of hearing "██████ stories" from the Superintendent, I questioned Mr. ██████ about ██████ and the Superintendent's relationship. Mr. ██████ informed me of several concerns, not the least of which was the general teacher perception about the relationship between the Superintendent and ██████. Mr. ██████ informed me at some point during the spring of academic year 2000-2001 that several incidents had taken place at the school which contributed to teacher perception of a negative nature. Mr. ██████ explained that ██████ was using a telephone in the Guidance office of ██████ ███████ Middle School to telephone Mr. ██████ on a daily basis. At that time, Mr. ██████ described ██████'s behavior in school as somewhat bizarre and pointed out that it had always been bizarre even prior to his relationship with the Superintendent. Mr. ██████ described how, during a building evacuation for a fire drill, ██████ bolted from the ranks of students to the Superintendent who had been seated in his car observing the fire drill. Mr. ██████ informed me that ██████ simply ran from his place on line with his class in the fire drill to the Superintendent's car to speak with the Superintendent who engaged him for some length in conversation rather than request his immediate return to his group. I was also told that teachers commented on this to Mr. ██████ along with negative comments on his use of the phone and other privileges that were noted as unusual and offensive. I asked

Mr. ████ if he discussed the perception teachers had of this relationship with Mr. ██████. He said "no." Just prior to school year 2000-2001, Mr. ██████ informed me that █████ had great fears about high school attendance, fears related to "getting beaten up... getting drowned by having his head held under water in a toilet bowl... and other unrealistic fears," according to the Superintendent. Then, for the first time, I realized we were not talking about a child with ████████ perceptions and behaviors. Prior to this, input from the Superintendent was primarily related to █████'s unusual politeness, exceptional interest in technology and other attributes of a more positive nature.

Prior to the close of the school 2000-2001, several teachers at the high school came to me to discuss their concerns about the Superintendent's relationship with ██████. They based their concerns on Middle School colleagues' observations and said they came to me because they felt I had a close relationship with the Superintendent and thought:

a) I could discuss the relationship with the Superintendent to ensure it did not continue at the High School and,

b) Might share with the Superintendent the negative perceptions ████ ████████ teachers had about the relationship.

Before figuring out how I might do either of these, as I had not ever met the child, Mr. ████████ asked me what I might do to ease the boy into the High School. I informed Mr. ██████ that █████ had been at the school with his eighth grade class for an orientation and that there would be another orientation in August, during the week just prior to school opening. Mr. ████████ felt this would not be enough to make ██████'s entry into ████ a smooth one because ███████ had fears that went beyond "the normal child's fears of high school."

I then informed Mr. ██████████ "many of the teachers at ████████ ████████████ felt the relationship was excessive and had suspicions of illicit behaviors based on the number of times the two interacted and based on ████████'s behaviors, speech and affect. Mr. ████████████ was upset by my presentation. I explained that I, as a colleague and friend was trying to prevent further rumors that might "damage" his career. I used the phrase, "they think you're in his pants."

Several weeks prior to the close of school year 2000-2001, the Superintendent asked me to give ███████ a "special tour" of the High School. I informed the Superintendent that I felt it would be inappropriate for me to do so. However, if he felt this child needed a special tour and introduction to the High School I would be willing to have one of our student guides or, perhaps, a monitor give him a tour. I told the Superintendent I did not want to establish a relationship with this child that would be based on his relationship with the Superintendent. Mr. ██████████ brought ███████ to the High School several weeks prior to the close of the school year, introduced him to me and asked if I would accompany them to the café as they had come during a lunch period. Mr. ████████████ informed me that ██████ was afraid of the café because of the crowds. I told Mr. ████████████ I would meet him in the lobby of the school (which is next to the café) and would arrange for a building tour led by someone other than myself. I subsequently met Mr. ██████████

and ███████ in the lobby and was introduced to ██████. It was immediately apparent to me that ██████████████████████████████████ ██. His presentation, affect, vocabulary and other soft signs bespoke ██████ ████████████████████████. He held out his hand to shake my hand in a very mature manner, kowtow in an Asian manner, darted his eyes back and forth around the lobby in a highly suspicious manner, and used words and phrases inappropriate to his age group, such as "I have heard so many positive things about you… it is my pleasure to make your acquaintance… thank you for arranging such a special tour…" and so on. I informed ███████ I would not be giving him his tour. He quickly looked at the Superintendent, whereupon I said, "It would be inappropriate for the principal to be a tour guide for every incoming student. You will have a tour from a school monitor." At that point, Mr. ██████████ asked if I would, at least, show ██████ the entrance to the cafeteria. The three of us approached the door. ███████ looked in, saw a student he feared and suddenly ran from us out the doors of the schools and into a nearby parking lot. I looked at the Superintendent who said, "I told you he was an unusual child." I accompanied the Superintendent out of the school toward ███████. I went about halfway to the child. The Superintendent continued and spoke with ███████. At some point that day, ██████ did have a tour of the building with a school monitor.

When the school year began, ███████ was immediately a very time-consuming, labor-intense, demanding, ████████████ student with ██████████ behaviors all of which were followed by references to the Superintendent, such as "I will report you to the Superintendent if you do not get this child to stop harassing me."

During the first weeks of the school year, I spoke with the Superintendent on a daily basis. This would not be unusual for the opening months of the school year, except each school-related discussion on the phone was followed by the Superintendent's queries about ███. I never telephoned the Superintendent regarding our problems with ███ which occurred every few days, particularly when he would antagonize students with his provocative behavior. But, I did answer his direct questions about ███. For example, when the Superintendent asked me "were there any problems with ███ today," I informed him that he created a disturbance during lunch in the café and had to be put in ILA (an in-school suspension room for ███████████ students). The Superintendent usually followed my comments about ███ with such comments as, "I thought I was making such good progress with him...I will have to discuss this with him... I told him not to do that anymore," and so on. It seemed that the Superintendent was having daily interactions with ███ during the opening weeks of the school year.

Shortly after the school year began, perhaps, within a few weeks, Mr. ██████ began visiting the school more regularly. Prior to this time, during my first three years at ███, he would come, of course, to visit if there were an emergency (bomb scare, fire, etc.) but did not visit except with a purpose of such nature. Maybe, he visited ten times a year. Now he was visiting several times a week, to see ███.

The current school year (2001-2002) began and within two months, many teachers at ███ started to have feelings similar to the teachers at ███ █████████. They expressed concern regarding the Superintendent's continuous visits to █████ in our school, seeing that he would visit our school several times a week and show up at █████'s classroom door. I expressed these concerns directly to Mr. ██████████ and, once again, advised him to start a District-wide mentoring program of which he could be the role model if this truly was a mentoring effort. I shared with him the teachers' and teaching assistants' concerns (and monitors) because █████ was continuously using the Superintendent's name. █████ had poor impulse control and exhibited ████████ behaviors aimed at others. As a result, he angered other students in classes, the café, and the corridor and created group scenes focused on himself. Whenever, he would be taken to an administrator or would have a problem with a teacher in class regarding his behavior, he would invoke Mr. █████████'s name. This began to grate on people more and more and I continued to share this with the Superintendent. "I can get you fired… I make daily reports on you to Mr. █████████… You handled that well, I'll tell the Superintendent…" I began to get phone calls from the Superintendent with questions about occurrences in the building that were reported to him by ██████. For example: Mr. ████████ called to ask me why I called the police and did not inform him (█████ erroneously thought there was an incident because he saw a police car). On another day, Mr. █████████ called to ask what the problem was with the parent who was angry with me (█████ saw a parent yelling at her child). This happened many times until I told Mr. █████████ to cease his reliance on █████ for information.

In November, I went to my immediate supervisor, Assistant Superintendent for Instruction, █████ █████████. I shared my concerns as well as those of others at ███. It was indicated that the District administration and other staff members at District headquarters were also concerned because ███ was reporting to the Superintendent's office several times a week after school. I was told by members of the Superintendent's cabinet that "all of us have discussed his relationship with ███ and that it doesn't look good."

In my next discussion about ███ with the Superintendent, at the beginning of December, I informed the Superintendent that ███'s behavior looked well beyond the Superintendent's ability to remedy. At that point, ███ was demonstrating ███ ███ behavior that was highly provocative. It can best be described as prancing in the café, lodging himself behind students who were seated at tables and wiggling fingers over their heads. He would do this repeatedly until the student became angry whereupon ███ would then turn into "the victim". This became such a regular occurrence that we often had to remove ███ from the café to have lunch in ILA with whatever teacher was on duty at that time. This occurred repeatedly and ███'s behaviors got worse. We discussed these behaviors with his father. In one such meeting, ███'s father said, "Let me remind you that I am his father." When I asked him to explain his statement, he said he did not want me to contact the Superintendent when ███ had a problem. He wanted me to contact him. I assured him I understood his role.

I mentioned the father's comments to the Superintendent. The Superintendent replied, "If he's the father why didn't he buy him school clothes, why didn't he take care of him better?" I asked him to what he was referring, and the Superintendent told me that he, himself, took ███ shopping during the week prior to school opening and bought him school clothes, including underwear. The Superintendent also told me, ███ was constantly leaving his house on weekends to come to the ███ residence. The Superintendent described to me that ███ was spending a great deal of time there. He told me that on weekend mornings, he and ███ would take a walk around the neighborhood and he described ███'s ███ need to speak with everyone as they walked. Again, I tried to inform the Superintendent about the public perceptions of his relationship with ███ as well as ███'s increasingly ███ behaviors in school. It had become apparent to us in school, with the insights of his school psychologist, Dr. ███ ███, that ███ was continuously misbehaving in order that the Superintendent come over to the school to rescue him from whatever punishment we would impose. This did, in fact, begin to occur regularly. When ███ was placed in ILA, the Superintendent would visit. This would occur after ███ would manage to sneak to a phone, to telephone the Superintendent that he "was being held prisoner against his will." On repeated occasions the Superintendent showed up at ███ during one of ███'s placement into ILA, lunch detention or other such punishment. He would go to ███, smilingly admonish him and, upon occasion, take him from the building. When I told Mr. ███ we could not figure out how he always knew when ███ was being punished, he just smiled. In all, the Superintendent probably took ███ from the building more than eight times between September-March. On one such occasion, I was out of the building at a meeting of county principals. Mr. ███ was in charge of the building. He telephoned me to inform me that the Superintendent came into the building without reporting to him and went directly to ███. Mr. ███ did not even know the Superintendent was in the building. He accidentally learned of his presence when Mr. ███ was walking in a corridor and crossed paths with the Superintendent who had taken ███ from ILA and was, again, leaving the building with him. Mr. ███ telephoned me to report this because he did not know whether this was permissible.

The next day, I again spoke with Superintendent about ███. I told him that ███'s behavior was getting more and more ███ and that he has begun enticing people to fight him. His café behaviors were intercepted by café monitors and others before he could cause major problems. This would often result in the Superintendent's immediate attendance. Now that we had begun to prevent those behaviors by placing ███ into permanent ILA-lunch, he began to antagonize the tough kids in the corridor, urging them to fight with him for no reason, whatsoever, except to get in trouble so the Superintendent would come and rescue him. I described these behaviors to the Superintendent. I also told the Superintendent that he seemed to be acting more and more ███. When I described ███'s ███ style to the Superintendent, the Superintendent told me, "He is not gay... he has some European affectations... he goes out with girls... he recently went out on a date with a girl and they ended up in her bed... the girl fell asleep... ███ pulled down the girl's pants and performed oral sex..." The Superintendent giggled and chuckled about ███'s sexual episode (or, what ███ told the Superintendent was his episode). The Superintendent also informed me that his own therapist had urged him to separate from ███████. I supported that and told him he should immediately sever this relationship before it ended up a "career buster." Mr. ████████ told me he was "trying to do that." He also told me that his wife and daughter wanted him to cut down on his time with ██████ and they did not want him at their home. Mr. █████████ informed me that he was trying to get his daughter, ████████, to assume a similar role with ██████'s younger sister.

During the mid-point of the school year, ██████'s father began picking him up after school. To some, this seemed like Dad's attempt to keep the boy away from the Superintendent. At about the same time, the mid-point of the school year, ██████ began to respond quite negatively to Dr. ████████'s ████████. This was largely due to the fact that Dr. ████████ was making demands on ██████ and confronting him about his ████████ behavior and the purpose for same (to attract attention to himself and to lure the Superintendent into the school). ██████ complained so bitterly to his father about Dr. ████████'s sessions and the fact that Dr. ████████ would make reference to his mother's departure and father's poor leadership skills that the father came to my office, demanding that ██████ no longer be seen by Dr. ████████. At that time, he also reiterated that he was the father of ██████ and that the Superintendent was not to be called if ██████ had any issues.

Made in the USA
Lexington, KY
15 July 2013